BADGER ASSEMBLY STORIES

WITH CITIZENSHIP AND PSHE THEMES

Ages 5-7

Andy and Barbara Seed

Badger Publishing
26 Wedgwood Way, Pin Green Industrial Estate, Stevenage, Hertfordshire SG1 4QF
Telephone: 01438 356907 Fax: 01438 747015

Cover photograph: Educational Solutions Ltd

INTRODUCTION

This book contains 25 assemblies for children aged 5-7, written specifically to resource the Non-statutory guidelines for PSHE and Citizenship at Key Stage 1. Each assembly begins with an introduction and then a main presentation, usually given by the teacher. There are both interactive and non-interactive follow-up ideas and every assembly concludes with an optional reflection or prayer. The assemblies use a wide range of stimulus material:

- Original stories
- Fiction: excerpts from children's books
- 'True life' stories: factual accounts of people's lives
- Factual accounts of events
- Information, e.g. the dangers of household products
- Mini drama sketches for children to perform, with play scripts
- Poems

Each assembly focuses on a single teaching requirement from the four strands of the PSHE and Citizenship guidelines, as listed in the contents and on the relevant assembly pages.

Follow up

Each assembly presentation is followed by suggestions for interaction to involve the audience in the assembly and to reinforce learning. Interactive follow up activities include:

- Closed and open questions
- Active response, e.g. vote, hands up, thumbs up or down, giving scores
- Quizzes
- Calling out answers to complete sentences
- Use of volunteers to assist at the front
- Discussion

Non-interactive follow up suggestions include:

- A summary of the story
- Points to think about
- Reflection and prayer

Using the material

The assemblies in the book are designed to be used flexibly: it is intended that teachers select the most appropriate follow up activities and questions from the range provided in order to meet the needs of the children present. The basic core presentation of each assembly may also be adapted to suit the school, of course, and may be used, for example, in circle time, as the basis for role-play or other drama or for classroom discussion in Citizenship lessons. Questions to stimulate response from the children might include:

- What might it feel like to be in this situation?
- Has anything like this ever happened to you?
- Why did the characters do what they did?
- Were they right/wrong?

What makes a successful assembly?

Good preparation is essential, particularly if drama is involved. Other key pointers:

- Use of props or a visual focus (suggestions are included in the book; don't forget an OHP or data projector can be used to show a picture if you can't find the object suggested).
- Relate the contents of the assembly to activities going on in the school or community.
- Interactivity: music, songs, drama or any kind of audience participation generates interest.
- Use the story or presentation to make a single clear learning point, which can be reinforced in the reflection or prayer at the end of the assembly.

CONTENTS

1A FAIR AND UNFAIR, RIGHT AND WRONG

Objective
To help children consider the importance of likes and dislikes, fair and unfair situations, and things that are right and wrong.

PSHE/Citizenship links
1a (Likes and dislikes etc), 1b (Sharing opinions)

Props
(Not essential): a packet of sweets and a piece of broccoli

Introduction
We all have things we like and dislike. We've all seen things that are fair and things that are unfair. And we all know things that are right and things that are wrong. Today's assembly starts with a story poem about a girl who got upset about two things: sweets and broccoli (hold up the objects).

POEM: KATIE'S TROUBLES

Katie was shopping
In town with her mum.
They walked past a sweetshop
"Ooooh," said Katie,
"Can I have some sweets?"
"Not today," said Mum.
"Aaawww, why not?"
"You had some yesterday Katie, that's why."
"That's not fair."
"Eating too many sweets is bad for your teeth."
"But I like sweets!"
"I like sweets too Katie, but
"We can't always have what we want, can we now?"
"Not fair."
"Not fair."
"Not fair."
Katie was in a miserable grump.
"Come on," said Mum, "let's go to the supermarket."
"What for?" said Katie.
"We need some vegetables for dinner tomorrow."
They bought broccoli.
"I don't like broccoli," said Katie.
"I know, but it's very good for you."
"It's horrid."
"I'll only give you a small piece, Katie."

"I don't want any."

"Just a small piece."

"Not fair."

"Not fair."

"Not fair."

"Please stop grumbling, Katie."

"No I won't!"

"Not fair."

"Not fair."

"Not fair."

INTERACTIVE FOLLOW UP ACTIVITIES

Questions

1) Why was Katie in a grump?

   (She couldn't have sweets.)

2) Why wouldn't Mum buy her any sweets?

   (She'd had some yesterday and too many sweets are bad for your teeth.)

3) Which two things did Katie think were unfair?

   (1. That she couldn't have sweets; 2. That she had to eat some broccoli.)

Likes and dislikes

a.   Hands up who likes sweets.

b.   Hands up who likes broccoli.

Fair and unfair

Katie didn't get any sweets – she thought this wasn't fair. Mum thought it was fair.

- Put your hand up if you thought it was fair that Katie didn't get any sweets.
- Put your hand up if you thought it was unfair.

Right and wrong

Whatever we like and whatever we think is fair, there are some things that are right and some things that are **wrong**. Mum was right to encourage Katie to eat healthy food. Katie was wrong to... Well, what did Katie do wrong?

(She said "No I won't" when Mum asked her to stop grumbling.)

Call out **right** or **wrong** for each of these:

- Being kind to animals.
- Crossing the road without looking.
- Listening to your teacher.
- Calling people rude names.
- Stealing.
- Helping someone who is hurt.
- Looking after your school work.

Non-interactive Follow Up

Summary of the poem
* Katie went shopping with her mum.
* Katie wanted some sweets.
* Mum said no and Katie said it wasn't fair.
* Mum bought some broccoli for Katie's dinner but Katie didn't want to eat it.
* Katie was grumpy and rude to her mum.

Something to think about
1) There are some things we *think* are not fair and some things that are *really* not fair.
2) Katie's mum wanted her to eat broccoli because it was good for her – our parents usually do what they think is best for us, even when we don't like it.
3) If you answer people in a rude, bad-tempered way – what will other people think of you?

Reflection
Try to do what is right, even if you think something is unfair. If you don't like something, there is usually a right way to say so and a wrong way to say so.

Prayer
Lord God, thank you that we have people like parents and teachers around us who want to do what's best for us. Please help me to do what is right, even when I think something is not fair. Help me not to say the wrong things, even when there is something I don't like. Help me to treat other people the right way. Amen.

1B SHARING OPINIONS

Objective

To help children learn the value of sharing opinions and explaining views on things that matter to them.

PSHE/Citizenship links

1b (Explaining views)

Props

(Not essential): a flat round plate and a ball

Introduction

The world is full of ideas. Some of them are good ideas and some of them are not so good. Sharing ideas, whether they are good or bad, is important. And so is talking about ideas. When you say whether you like an idea or not, this is called 'sharing your opinion'. Today's story is about a man with an idea that many people laughed at, until he proved them all wrong.

TRUE STORY: FALLING OFF THE WORLD

The planet that we live on, the Earth, is round, like a ball. Everyone knows that. astronauts in space have taken photographs of Earth, which show that it is round. But a long time ago – five hundred years ago or more – many people thought that the world was flat. They believed that it was shaped like a giant plate.

A few people in those days thought that the world was round, but not many. One of them was a sailor. He was called Christopher Columbus. Columbus believed that the world was round and he wanted to explore it. He had heard about explorers who had travelled across land for thousands of miles and reached wonderful places in the east like India and China. These explorers brought back silk, which people in Europe, where Christopher Columbus lived, had never seen. They also brought back spices and gold.

Christopher Columbus wanted to go to the east. He wanted to find more silk and spices and gold. But it took people travelling across land years to reach places like China. Christopher Columbus thought it would be much quicker to sail there, but the trouble was that no one had found how to reach the east by sea. The giant continent of Africa was in the way!

Christopher Columbus thought about this problem a lot. He studied maps and charts and he watched ships sailing out to sea. He thought that the world was round and that he could perhaps sail to the west. "If I keep going," he thought, "I will sail around the world and get to the east!" He dreamt about the riches of the east for many years.

Christopher Columbus told some people about his idea of sailing to the west and going around the world. Most people laughed at him.

"Christopher Columbus – you are a fool," they said. "The Earth is flat. If you sail to the west and keep on going you will come to the edge of the world and fall off!"

But these people didn't put Christopher Columbus off his idea. He made plans to sail with three ships to find a new route to the east. He would fill his ships with gold and bring it back to Europe. The trouble was that an expedition like this cost a huge amount of money. There were the ships to pay for, and the men to sail in them, and the food and all the equipment. Christopher Columbus didn't have much money. How would he ever afford to make his special voyage?

He decided to go and see a Spanish queen called Isabella. It took a long time to convince people but eventually the king and queen gave Christopher Columbus enough money to buy the ships and other things he needed for his voyage of discovery.

So, in the year 1492, Christopher Columbus set off across the mighty Atlantic Ocean, sailing west with three little wooden ships. Many of the people who saw him go thought that he was mad. They still believed the Earth was flat.

For ten weeks the ships sailed across the sea. Most of the men on board were very scared – no one had ever sailed this far before. Eventually, land was spotted – a small island. The ship sailed towards it and Christopher Columbus and his men went ashore with great excitement. They thought they had reached the east.

In fact, Christopher Columbus was a very long way from the east. He had found one of the islands of the Caribbean Sea near America. Later, he sailed further and found more islands and also reached South America.

Christopher Columbus never did reach the east, but he was right that it is possible to sail west to reach it. And he was right that the Earth is round like a ball and not flat. He returned to Spain with a little gold and no spices or silk. But he had made a great discovery.

INTERACTIVE FOLLOW UP ACTIVITIES

Questions

1) Why do you think most people believed the Earth was flat a long time ago?

   (It didn't look round from where they stood; there was no proof that it was round; they thought they would fall off if it was round, etc.)

2) Christopher Columbus was right about one thing and wrong about another – what were these two things?

   (He was right that the world is round and wrong that he had found the east.)

3) Who did listen to Christopher Columbus and believe that he was right?

   (The Spanish king and queen.)

Getting the message
1) What can we learn from this true story?

   (That we should listen to each other; that some opinions may be right and others may be wrong; that we should speak up for what we believe is right.)

2) Christopher Columbus explained to other people what he thought was right. He shared his views even when other people laughed at him. I'm going to read out some statements about saying what you think. Put your hand up if these are true for you:
   - I try to answer questions in class.
   - I try to speak when we talk about things in discussion time.
   - I listen to other people when they speak.
   - I can explain what I am thinking.
   - I speak when other people are speaking.
   - I speak loud and clear so everyone in the room can hear me.

Learning more
1) What does 'giving your opinion' mean?
2) Are the things people say always right or wrong?

NON-INTERACTIVE FOLLOW UP

Summary of the assembly
- 500 years ago most people thought that the world was flat like a plate.
- The sailor Christopher Columbus believed that the Earth was round.
- Christopher Columbus wanted to sail to the east by sailing west and going around the world.
- Many people thought he was mad but a Spanish king and queen gave him money for ships to go on his voyage.
- Christopher Columbus sailed across the Atlantic Ocean and discovered many islands and later found America.
- Christopher Columbus did not find a way to sail to the east but he did discover that the world is not flat and that you can't sail off the edge.

Something to think about
1) Why is it good to share your views and say what you think in class?
2) Why is it important to listen to other people?

Reflection
Remember brave Christopher Columbus, who sailed to America when most people thought he was completely wrong. Try to be brave like him and say what you believe is right, even when other people disagree.

Prayer
Lord God, thank you for Christopher Columbus and for all that he discovered. Help us to be brave like him in speaking up for what we believe is right, even when other people disagree or laugh at us. Amen.

1c Feelings

Objective

To help children understand how to recognise, name and deal with feelings in a positive way.

PSHE/Citizenship links

1c (Recognising, naming and dealing with feelings)

Props

(Not essential): a babygro and a rattle; for follow-up: several blank pieces of card and a thick, dark marker pen

Introduction

We all have feelings. Some are nice, but some aren't very good at all. Sometimes we can feel angry, jealous or afraid. The worst thing is when we feel like that, but we don't know why, and we don't know what to do about it. Listen to this true story about a little girl who had all sorts of different feelings. These things might give you a bit of a clue what the story's about *(hold up babygro and rattle)*.

TRUE STORY: I DON'T FEEL RIGHT

Chloe was a lovely little girl. She always seemed to be happy and she had lots of friends. If anyone looked sad at school, it would be Chloe who went to cheer them up; if there was someone who looked lonely, it would be Chloe who asked them to join in whatever game she was playing at playtime; if someone had done really well at something, Chloe was always the first to be pleased for them and to say "Well done!" Chloe had a really kind heart and was never mean to anybody. She also had a big family who all loved her.

Chloe was seven at the time of this story and had two brothers, Tom and Isaac, who were much bigger than her – they both went to the big school down the road and were nearly as tall as their dad. They were older than some of you sitting in this room today, when she was born, and they helped mum to take care of her when she was a tiny baby. Now they would often give her piggybacks and look after her if their mum had to go out. Chloe just loved having two big brothers and she loved being the smallest in the family.

One of the things that Chloe and her brothers enjoyed the most was visiting their Granny and Grandpa. Ever since she'd been born, Grandpa would say "Hello, Littlest!" when he saw Chloe and Chloe liked that, because it made her feel very special.

One weekend Chloe, her brothers and her Mum and Dad went to visit Granny and Grandpa. Chloe's Auntie Chris and Uncle John were there too. Auntie Chris had a big smile on her face. She said to them all, "I've been dying to get you all together like this, because we've got something very special to tell you. Uncle John and I are going to have a baby next year!" It all went quiet for a second, while the family took in the news, and then suddenly everyone was laughing, jumping up and down, and hugging Auntie Chris and Uncle John.

"That's fantastic news! When's it due? Do you want a boy or a girl? What will you call it? Brilliant!" Everyone talked at once. When the excitement had died down a bit, Chloe found herself standing by Grandpa. "It's good news for you, too!" he beamed, as he hugged her, "because you won't be the Littlest anymore!"

Chloe smiled at him and then went into the dining room, where her mum and Auntie Chris were talking as they laid the table for lunch. It was going to be one of Granny's special HUGE roast dinners with chicken, roast AND mashed potatoes, more yummy vegetables than you could possibly imagine, dozens of Yorkshire puddings and enough gravy to float a ship on.

Soon it was time for lunch and everyone was tucking in. Mum noticed that Chloe was just picking at her food. She hardly ate anything, even though it was her favourite kind of meal, and she didn't want any pudding either. She was very, very quiet for the rest of the afternoon too. "Oh dear!" she said to Dad, "I don't think that poor Chloe's feeling too well – she's off her food and she's not normally this quiet."

"Yes," agreed Dad, "she's either a bit over-tired or she's coming down with a bug, so I think we'd better get her home quite soon."

They said goodbye and went back home, with everyone still chatting excitedly about the new baby in the car. Everyone except poor Chloe, that is, who was still very quiet and wasn't looking at all good. When they got home, they popped her into bed early, and that must have done the trick, because she wasn't poorly after all and was fine to go to school the next morning.

Over the next few months, Auntie Chris and Uncle John were busy moving into a new house and getting everything ready for the baby. It was all very exciting. Gradually, though, Mum began to notice something a bit strange. Chloe didn't seem to join in with the excitement quite as much as she thought she would. She just didn't seem very interested.

Several months later, the time came for Auntie Chris and Uncle John's baby to be born. When the phone call came to say that baby Michael had arrived, Mum whooped for joy and everyone came running to hear the news. When she'd put the phone down, she noticed that Chloe had disappeared into the garden.

Mum left her for a minute or two and then followed her. She found that Chloe was in floods of tears. "Oh dear! Whatever's the matter, Chloe?" said Mum.

"I don't know!" sobbed Chloe. "I just feel all horrible inside, and I don't know why!"

Mum suddenly understood what was the matter and smiled. "I think I know EXACTLY what the problem is! Tell me a bit about how you feel."

"Oh Mum! I can't describe it! I feel all mean and nasty inside – and I shouldn't, should I? I should be really pleased that Auntie Chris has had a baby, like everyone else is, but I just don't – and somehow that makes it all even worse! I don't ever want to see him, and if I do I think I might be mean to him. I think I've turned into a horrible person!"

"No you haven't, you great dope!" laughed Mum. "You're one of the kindest, nicest people I know! You haven't suddenly changed! You're just a little bit jealous of the new baby, that's all."

Chloe gasped. "But Mum! Being jealous is a REALLY horrid thing, isn't it?"

"Well, Chloe," said Mum, giving her a big hug. "Sometimes we just can't help what we feel. The important thing is to know what to do about our feelings when we have them. Some feelings can be very strong and we need to understand them before we can do something about them. Can you remember the very first time you felt like you do now?"

Chloe started sobbing again. "Yes, it was when Grandpa said that I wasn't going to be the Littlest anymore! I felt so sad, because I thought it meant that I wouldn't be so special anymore and that he wouldn't love me as much when the new baby was born."

"But Chloe," explained Mum, "Grandpa doesn't love you or think you're special just because you've always been the littlest in the family! We all love you and think you're special because you're YOU. No one's going to stop loving you just because you've got a new baby cousin now! Do you think that we all stopped loving Tom and Isaac and thinking that they were special just because you came along? Of course not!"

"So," sniffed Chloe, "Granny and Grandpa still love me just as much as they did before Michael was born?"

"Of course they do, you big Nellie! We all do. The only thing that's changed is that there's an extra little person for *all* of us to love. And I bet he'll love having you as a big cousin. You can help to look after him just like the boys look after you."

"Oh wow! Will Michael love me just as much as I love my big brothers, then?" Chloe gasped.

"I'm sure of it!" laughed Mum.

"Well when can we go and see him? Can we go today? Oh, I can't wait!" spluttered Chloe. "And can I get him a present just from me, to let him know how special he is? Being the littlest in a family is a very special thing, you know!"

INTERACTIVE FOLLOW UP ACTIVITIES

Questions

1) What sort of a girl was Chloe?
   (Kind hearted, generous, helpful, caring, etc.)
2) Who was in Chloe's family?
   (Mum, Dad, brothers Tom & Isaac. Also Granny, Grandpa, Auntie Chris and Uncle John.)
3) Can you remember what Grandpa used to say to Chloe every time he saw her?
   ("Hello Littlest!")

Getting the message

1) How did Chloe feel about the baby at first?
   (She was JEALOUS.)
2) What helped her to feel better?
   (She talked to her mum about her feelings, and Mum reassured her.)
3) How did the story end?
   (Chloe got rid of her jealous feelings and was looking forward to seeing the baby.)

Learning more

1) There are lots of different types of feelings that we have. Who can think of some more? *(E.g. love, hate, joy, sadness, fear, anger, etc.)* Ask each child who volunteers an idea to come up to the front. Write the name of the feeling onto a piece of paper/card as they come out and give it to them to hold up.

2) Some of these feelings make us feel good (draw a big smiley face on a piece of card and ask for another volunteer to hold it up) and some make us feel bad inside (draw a big sad face on a piece of card and ask for another volunteer to hold it up.)

3) Let's see if we can put these feelings here into two groups. Ask children who have come out one by one to remind everyone what their feeling was and then ask everybody who is still sitting down, "Give me a thumbs up sign if that's a nice feeling to have, or a thumbs down sign if it's not a nice feeling to have." Send all those with 'positive' feelings to stand by the child with the smiley face sign and all those with 'negative' feelings to stand by the child with the sad face sign.

NON-INTERACTIVE FOLLOW UP

Summary of the story

- Chloe is a kind girl and is the youngest in a loving family.
- Grandpa always calls her "Littlest" and being the youngest makes her feel special.
- Her Auntie Chris and Uncle John have a new baby.
- Everyone is thrilled except Chloe, who can't understand why she isn't.
- She tells Mum about her feelings and Mum helps her to sort them out.
- She is able to leave the feelings of jealousy behind her and look forward to meeting the new baby.

Something to think about

1) Have you ever been jealous of anybody?
2) Was it a nice feeling?
3) Who could you talk to about your feelings if you feel angry, sad, scared or jealous?
4) Which is worse: having bad feelings about someone or actually doing something mean to them?

Reflection

Everyone has feelings: some are nice to have and others are not nice to have at all. If you are feeling bad about something, see if you can find someone to talk to about your feelings and help you feel better. Remember that it's not naughty to have bad feelings sometimes, but it is important not to do mean things to others just because you feel bad about something.

Prayer

Lord God, thank you that you made us able to have feelings. We love feelings like happiness, but sometimes we need help if we feel angry or jealous or scared. Please help us to sort out our feelings, so that we can be kind and helpful, not mean, to everyone around us. Amen.

1d RECOGNISING STRENGTHS

Objective
To help children think about themselves and recognise what they are good at.

PSHE/Citizenship links
1d (Thinking about themselves), 4c (Differences between people)

Props
(Not essential): some bean bags, a paintbrush and some paint

Introduction
All of us are different. We are all good at some things and not so good at others. Listen to this story about two girls who learnt something about themselves one day at school. These are a clue to some of the things that happen (hold up props). See if you can spot where they come into the story.

STORY: I'M NO GOOD AT THAT!

Becky loved PE lessons. She loved anything to do with running and jumping, throwing and catching and moving about. She loved it because she was good at it. Everyone always wanted Becky to be in their team, because Becky's team usually won. Well, today Becky's class were in the hall, ready to start their PE lesson, and Becky couldn't wait.

"Right," said Miss Jarvis. "Today we're going to have some fun with bean bags. We're going to see how good we are at throwing and catching. I'm going to put you into pairs, and I want you to practice throwing a bean bag to each other and catching it."

The children found partners and were given a bean bag. Becky was standing next to Mai Ling, so Miss Jarvis told them to work together. She gave them a bean bag and they moved into a space to start their throwing and catching. Becky threw the beanbag to Mai Ling, but Mai Ling dropped it. She picked it up and threw it back to Becky. Well, she tried to throw it back, but somehow it ended up going backwards, right over her own head, and nowhere near Becky at all. She scuttled off to pick it up and tried again.

The longer the lesson went on, the worse things got for Mai Ling. She just couldn't get the hang of either the throwing or the catching and she began to look very miserable. But things were about to get even worse than that.

Miss Jarvis blew her whistle. "Right, class! Well done, I've seen some lovely throwing and catching this morning. Now, who would like to show us how good they are?"

Before she'd really thought about how hard Mai Ling had found it, Becky's hand flew up. "Well done, Becky – let's see you and your partner, then."

Poor Mai Ling went bright red and stayed sitting down, but Becky was already up on her feet. There was nothing Mai Ling could do, but to get up and try her best. She'd had enough trouble when no one else had been watching, but now, in front of the whole class, she was even worse at it. She dropped every single bean bag that Becky threw and couldn't throw them back to Becky at all. When they sat down, she felt hot tears stinging her eyes.

15

"Never mind, Mai Ling," said Miss Jarvis kindly. "Better luck next time." But Mai Ling did mind. She felt completely useless. She was very quiet for the rest of the morning and didn't enjoy her dinner one bit, even though it was her favourite.

When the children got back into the classroom after dinner, all of the tables were covered in newspaper and there were paintbrushes, paints and pots of water out on each of them. That cheered Mai Ling up a bit, because she enjoyed painting. Before long, she was working hard on a beautiful painting of a garden. It had flowers, grass, swings for children to play on and some lovely trees with shiny red apples on it. She was working so hard that she hardly noticed what was going on around her.

She looked up just as she was mixing a wonderful bright yellowy green for the leaves of the apple trees and noticed that Becky was sitting very quietly and miserably in front of her piece of paper. When Mai Ling looked at the picture Becky had painted, all she could see was a sort of brownish splodge, with a few blobs of a nasty sludgy green dotted about. Miss Jarvis had noticed too.

"What's the matter, Becky?" she asked, as she came over to Becky's table.

"Oh Miss Jarvis, just look at this! I know exactly what I want to paint – I've got it all in my head, but I just can't make it go right on the paper! I've made a horrible mess!" The tears started to fall down her cheeks.

Mai Ling felt very sorry for her. That was just how she'd felt that morning, when she couldn't throw and catch properly. She went over to Becky and put her arm round her shoulder. "Don't worry - I know just how you feel!" she said.

Becky sniffed. "But how can you know how I feel – just look at your beautiful picture. It's lovely and mine's so horrid!"

"Remember what happened this morning with the bean bags?" said Mai Ling. "I felt so useless, because I just couldn't do it at all. It was even worse because I was your partner, and you're so good at that sort of thing!"

Becky began to dry her tears. "But you're not useless, Mai Ling – just look at how well you can paint!"

"Yes!" laughed Mai Ling, "and you're not useless either – just look how well you can throw and catch!"

"That's right," smiled Miss Jarvis. "Neither of you is useless at all. You are both just good at different things. And anyway, neither of you is useless at the other things either – maybe you just need a bit more practice."

Becky smiled for the first time that afternoon. "I suppose *all* of us are good at different things – we just need to find out what it is we're good at. Mai Ling – as you're so good at painting, will you teach me how to get better at it, please?"

"I will," grinned Mai Ling, "as long as you help me to get better at throwing and catching!"

16

INTERACTIVE FOLLOW UP ACTIVITIES

Questions

1) What sort of lessons did Becky really enjoy?

   (PE and Games)

2) Who can remember what the class had to do in their PE lesson?

   (Throwing and catching bean bags.)

3) What was Becky's partner called?

   (Mai Ling)

4) Did Mai Ling enjoy her PE lesson?

   (No – because she was very bad at throwing and catching.)

5) Did Becky enjoy her painting lesson?

   (No – because she was so bad at painting.)

Getting the message

1) What can we learn from this story?

   (We are all good at different things; it's good to be kind to people who may not be so good at something as you are: they might be able to help you with something you can't do.)

2) We usually enjoy doing the things that we're good at, like the girls in the story.

   • Give me a thumbs-up if you enjoy PE and Games lessons, like Becky.

   • Give me a thumbs-up if you enjoy painting and drawing, like Mai Ling.

   • Who can think of other things we do in school? *(Ask for a thumbs-up if they enjoy each one of the suggestions.)*

Learning more

1) It's not just at school that we can be good at different things. Have a think about things that you do after school, or at weekends. Can anyone tell us about something that they enjoy doing out of school? *(Examples: Rainbows or Beavers, sports clubs, e.g. football, gymnastics, dancing, swimming etc.)*

2) And what about at home? What sort of things can you be good at, at home? *(Examples: helping, playing with brothers and sisters without arguing, being kind and thinking of other people, saying please and thank you, keeping your room tidy, etc.)* Being good at those sorts of things is just as important as being good at things you do in school.

NON-INTERACTIVE FOLLOW UP

Summary of the story

- Becky loved PE lessons and was good at them, but Mai Ling found throwing and catching very difficult.
- Mai Ling got very upset about it.
- In the afternoon there was painting. This time Becky got upset because she couldn't do it so well and Mai Ling enjoyed herself because she was so good at painting.
- Miss Jarvis helped them to realise that they were just good at different things and the girls promised to help each other.

Something to think about

1) Think of three things that you can do really well.
2) Think of something that you're not so good at.
3) Have a think about your friends: are they good at different things too?

Reflection

Don't be upset if there are things that you can't do so well. Just try hard and do your best with everything you do. Think of the things that you can do really well and it won't seem so bad. If you see someone struggling with something that they find difficult, be kind to them.

Prayer

Lord God, thank you that you made us all to be good at different things. Please help us to do the best we can with things we find hard and remind us of the things we are good at. Help us to help each other throughout the day. Amen.

1e SETTING GOALS

Objective
To help children understand what it means to set goals and how they can be achieved.

PSHE/Citizenship links
1e (Setting simple goals)

Props
(Not essential): an empty medicine bottle

Introduction
If you really want to do something then you can ask other people to help you. But there are some things you can only do yourself. Sometimes, the only way to do something is to set yourself a target and to try and try by working hard. Today's assembly is the true story of a remarkable person who did just that. But what did he want to do? *(Hold up the object.)*

TRUE STORY: ALBERT SCHWEITZER

Some people are born clever. Some people grow up to be great musicians, some people grow up to be successful writers and some people grow up to be important speakers who teach others. Just occasionally, once in a while, someone very special comes along who can do all of these. Albert Schweitzer was such a man. He was from Germany but he became famous all over the world.

Albert learnt to play the organ, a keyboard instrument, at a young age and soon became very good. He gave concerts all over Europe. When Albert wasn't playing music, he was preaching in church or writing books. Albert was also good at teaching people about the things he enjoyed and he was offered a job at a great university in France. There were so many things for the talented Albert to do, that he was always busy.

Then, one day, Albert was reading a book. It was about Africa and it told of the way that many thousands of people in Africa died from diseases because there were not enough doctors, nurses and hospitals. Albert decided that he needed to help these poor people who were much less fortunate than him. The trouble was that Albert was not a doctor and knew very little about medicine. But he set himself a goal – a target – he would learn to become a doctor.

It took six years. Six years of hard work and exams and tests. But Albert Schweitzer became a doctor. As soon as he could, he made plans to go to Africa. Albert's friends in Europe thought he was crazy, because in those days, about a hundred years ago, Africa was a very dangerous place to visit.

The place where Albert went, now called Gabon, was hot and full of disease. There were no hospitals, so Albert decided to build one. He had no one to help him and no money to pay for a proper building so he used a hen house. Albert cleaned it up and found a table to put his bottles of medicine on. People soon started coming to Albert, the white doctor, for help. Two thousand people were treated and helped in the first year he was there – the Africans came to trust Albert because they saw that he cared for them.

19

The hen hut hospital wasn't big enough for all of the patients who needed help, so Albert set himself another goal – another target – to put up a bigger, better building. He asked for help and it came. Soon there was somewhere cleaner and safer to work, and more staff to help Albert.

Albert needed to buy more medicines and bandages and other medical equipment for operations, so he set himself another goal, to raise money to help more people. To do this, he went back to Europe and played musical concerts. He told people about his work with the poor and the sick and people gave him lots of money. Albert went back to Africa and built a better hospital. More doctors and nurses came to help – these were people who had heard all about the wonderful work that Albert was doing.

Albert continued to help people in Africa for many years until he became an old man and died. He had reached all of his goals.

INTERACTIVE FOLLOW UP ACTIVITIES

Questions
1) What things was Albert Schweitzer good at?
   (Music, writing, teaching, preaching, helping others, medicine.)
2) Why did he go to Africa?
   (He read that people there were dying because of a lack of medical care and he wanted to help them.)
3) Albert set himself goals or targets – what does that mean?
   (Something to aim for; things that he wanted to try to do.)

Put your hand up if I say something that was a goal of Albert Schweitzer:
- To help people in Africa. ✓
- To become a doctor. ✓
- To buy himself a big house.
- To build a hospital. ✓
- To live an easy life and get rich.

Setting goals
Sometimes, it's a good idea if we set ourselves goals, targets that we can try for. Here are some:
- Playing with someone who is on their own at playtime.
- Reading at home.
- Trying really hard to listen to the teacher in class.

Remembering the story:
Call out the missing words.
- There was a clever man from Germany called Albert _____ . *(Schweitzer)*
- Albert wanted to help poorly people in _____ . *(Africa)*
- Albert became a doctor and built a _____ . *(hospital)*
- Albert set himself targets to reach; you can also set yourself _____ . *(targets)*
- Albert reached his goals by caring and by working _____ . *(hard)*

20

NON-INTERACTIVE FOLLOW UP

Summary of the story

- Albert Schweitzer was a very clever, talented man.
- He was a musician, writer, teacher and church leader.
- One day Albert found out that many people in Africa were dying of diseases.
- Albert decided to become a doctor and to go to Africa to help them.
- Albert built a hospital and helped many thousands of poor Africans.
- Albert set himself goals and he reached them by hard work.

Something to think about

1) It's a good idea to set yourself a simple target or goal sometimes.
2) Your goal could be to help someone.
3) Another kind of target is to work hard at school to improve your reading or writing.

Reflection

Learn from the story of Albert Schweitzer who gave up so much to help others. Learn from the way he set himself goals to reach and then worked towards them.

Prayer

Lord God, thank you for great people like Albert Schweitzer. Help me to be kind to others like him. Help me to set goals and targets that I can reach, especially with my work at school. Help me to keep trying until I succeed. Amen.

2A Taking Part in Discussions

Objective
To help children recognise the value of taking part in discussions in the classroom.

PSHE/Citizenship links
2a (Taking part in discussions)

Props
(Not essential): a photograph of the Amazon Rainforest, displayed with an OHP or data projector. *(You can find pictures at www.google.com by clicking the 'images' tab and searching.)*

Introduction
Do you join in discussions in the classroom? A discussion is when everyone gets the chance to talk about something and to listen to each other. Some people like to say a lot and others keep very quiet. Here's a story about a class who had a discussion about something very interesting.

Story: Save the Rainforest!

Mr Karelski, Class 2's teacher, told everyone to sit on the carpet while he set up the TV.

"Right, Class, I'm going to show you a video now all about the Amazon Rainforest. The Amazon Rainforest is the biggest jungle in the world. It's a very special place – I've been there myself – but something very sad is happening to it. So, let's watch the video and then we'll talk about it at the end."

The video was called 'Amazon in Danger'. It started with some film of beautiful, bright coloured macaws, which are large parrots, flying through tall treetops in the rainforest. Then the children saw what the jungle looked like from high in the air – it was like an enormous lumpy carpet of green with a few brown rivers snaking between the trees.

Then there were pictures of what it was like on the ground – quite dark, with lots of dangling creepers trailing from the trees. There were close ups of ants and giant beetles and monkeys and alligators and lots and lots of birds.

The video's narrator told the children some amazing facts about the Amazon Rainforest – about how big it is and how many thousands of animals live there. She also said that there are very few people living in this part of the world.

Then there were pictures of some of the tribes who have lived in the Amazon for hundreds of years. These are people who live simple lives without technology. Some of them still survive just by hunting and fishing in the rivers and by searching for berries and roots to eat. They are experts at how to live in the jungle and how to look after it.

But then the children of Class 2 were shocked to see a picture of something they really didn't expect to see. An enormous roaring yellow bulldozer was pushing over trees and scraping away the bushes and greenery, to leave wide open spaces of raw red soil. Then there were pictures of men with chainsaws cutting into the trunks of the bigger trees, which came crashing to the ground with the ear-splitting sound of huge branches bending and snapping.

The narrator on the video explained that big areas of the rainforest were being cut down and cleared. There were three reasons for this, she said. First, the timber or wood from the trees was worth a lot of money, so people were selling it to build houses and furniture. Second, farmers were clearing away the forest to make open spaces for cattle to graze and to grow crops like bananas to sell. And lastly, in some places, people were digging into the ground to try to find valuable minerals like precious metals.

Next it was explained how quickly the Amazon Rainforest was being cut down and how many of the wild animals were losing their homes.

"The rainforest tribes are also having their land stolen," the narrator said. "Much of the timber that is cut down is also burned, causing pollution."

A few minutes later the video was over and Mr Karelski asked everyone to sit in a circle.

"Right children, we're going to have a discussion now about the Amazon Rainforest. In a discussion, everyone has a chance to say something but only one person can speak at a time, so you must put up your hand. And the other thing you must do is listen. So, the question is, do you think it's right that people are allowed to cut down parts of the Amazon Rainforest?"

About half of the children put up their hands right away. Mr Karelski began to ask people to speak.

"I don't think it's right," said Gemma, "because animals like birds and monkeys are losing their homes."

"And they might get killed from all the trees falling and the fires," said Samuel.

"I think the pollution is very bad too," said Yoka.

"It's not fair that the people with the bulldozers are stealing the land because it really belongs to the tribes," said Jozef.

"I think it's bad to cut it down because the jungle is beautiful," said Reece.

"That's right," said Mr Karelski, "it is beautiful – and if it's all cut down then none of you will be able to visit it like I did. There were some very good points made there, Class 2, well done. But does anyone disagree with any of the things that have just been said?" No hands went up. "Well, can anyone think of any reasons why people should be allowed to cut down part of the rainforest." This time, a couple of hands went up.

"If the people can sell the wood then they can make some money for their families," said Michael.

"That's true," said Mr Karelski. "Clearing the forest does provide jobs for people. Any thing else?"

"The video said that farmers were growing crops on the land – so maybe the people need more food," said Su-Lin.

"That's another good point," said the teacher. "There are cities in Brazil with millions of people in them who all need to be fed."

"But can't they grow crops on other land or buy food from other countries?" said Yoka.

More hands went up and the interesting discussion continued. A few minutes later, Mr Karelski told the children to put their hands down. It was nearly the end of the lesson.

© Badger Publishing Ltd.

There was only one child who had not said anything at all – Nathan. Mr Karelski knew that Nathan was a very quiet boy, who hardly ever put up his hand. He was also much more interested in cars than animals and the jungle. "Oh well," thought Mr Karelski to himself, "it's a shame that we don't know what Nathan thinks about this, but you can't force someone to talk if they don't want to."

Mr Karelski then gave everyone a piece of paper and a book and asked the children to draw an animal that lives in the jungle. Su-Lin wanted to draw the big spotted jungle cat which was on the cover of her book, but it didn't say what type of cat it was. Mr Karelski asked the class.

"I know." It was Nathan. "It's a jaguar. I know because my next door neighbour has a Jaguar car and the metal badge looks like that."

"You're right Nathan, well done," said the teacher.

"But why is a car named after a cat?" said Su-Lin.

"I think it's because it's fast and looks good," said Nathan.

Mr Karelski smiled – it looked like another discussion was starting.

INTERACTIVE FOLLOW UP ACTIVITIES

Questions

1) Why did Mr Karelski show his class a video about the Amazon rainforest?
   (To start off a discussion.)
2) What were the rules for the discussion that Mr Karelski told the class?
   (Only one person at a time may talk, anyone can join in, put up hands, everyone listens.)
3) Did everyone join in the discussion?
   (Nathan didn't at first, but he started a new discussion at the end.)

Getting the message

1) During a discussion, are people allowed to disagree with each other? *(Yes)*
2) What does 'giving your opinion' mean? *(Saying what you think or believe.)*
3) Show if you agree or disagree with these statements about discussion. Put your thumb up for the ones you agree with and thumb down for the ones you disagree with:
   - You should always agree with your friends in a discussion.
   - It is important to listen to other people in a discussion.
   - Shouting in discussions is a good idea.
   - People should only be allowed to speak once in a discussion.
   - Everyone should try and join in a class discussion.

Learning more

1) Do you ever have discussions at home? What sort of things do you discuss?
2) The government have discussions in places like parliament. What are these for?
   (To help decide how the country should be run.)

NON-INTERACTIVE FOLLOW UP

Summary of the story
- Mr Karelski's class had a discussion about the Amazon Rainforest.
- They started off by watching a video so they knew something about it.
- Mr Karelski explained how a discussion works.
- He asked the class whether they thought it was right for the rainforest to be cut down.
- The children discussed this question, coming up with arguments for and against it.
- Nathan didn't say anything until the end, when he started a new discussion about cats and cars.

Something to think about
1) Do you always try and join in discussions in the classroom?
2) What is good about discussions?

Reflection
Discussions are very important. When we have a discussion we share ideas and learn what other people think. We also start to get more ideas of our own and learn how to say things in front of other people. Try and join in discussions whenever you can.

Prayer
Lord God, thank you that you gave us brains to think and mouths to speak. Thank you that we can learn to discuss questions in school and learn from each other as we listen. Help us to join in discussions and to think hard about the things we say. Amen.

2b Taking Part in Debate

Objective
To help children understand why taking part in debate is important.

PSHE/Citizenship links
2b (Taking part in a simple debate about topical issues)

Props
(Not essential): a padlock

Introduction
Today's assembly is all about why it is important to talk about the things that are going on in the world. It tells the story of a man who found that talking was like a key, which could open locks (*hold up the padlock*).

TRUE STORY: WILLIAM WILBERFORCE

Try to imagine this: a man is at home, resting after a hard day's work. Suddenly, there is a crash and the door flies open. Four large men rush into the room and grab the other man. They tie his hands together and take him outside. He is put in a truck and driven away to a strange place. He is not told where he is being taken. He never sees his family again.

This is unlikely to happen today, but if you were a man or woman living in Africa two hundred years ago, this could easily have happened to you. People were captured and taken from their homes. They were tied up with chains, which were often fixed around their necks, and they were forced to walk miles to a place where they would be taken even further away. Most of them never saw their families again. These people had become slaves.

Two hundred years ago, millions of African people were taken away like this to become slaves. They were loaded on board large wooden sailing ships and cramped together, still chained up, below the decks. It was dark and smelly. The slaves were often sick and always hungry and very uncomfortable. Many of them died on these sea voyages.

But where were these African slaves being taken? Many were taken to America where they were sold, just as if they were something in a shop, like food or clothes or toys. The people who bought them were rich white men – slave owners and traders. So the African men and women found that they were in a strange country and that they now belonged to someone they didn't know.

The slaves did not understand the language. They were treated with cruelty and given very little to eat or drink. Then they were forced to work – most worked on farms doing jobs such as picking cotton in the fields. It was hot, hard, back-breaking work. The slaves were not paid for this work and were given very little time for rest. Some tried to run away – they were soon caught and punished.

This seems very cruel to us today. We know that slavery is wrong. But two hundred years ago, most white people thought that there was nothing wrong with slavery – it was just another business. Many people in Britain in those days didn't know what life was like for slaves – there were no TV pictures to show them and photographs hadn't been invented. News travelled very slowly, and most people in this country didn't care about slaves anyway.

But some people did. Some people in Britain found out what life was like for slaves. They felt strongly that it was wrong and that it should be stopped. One of these people was a man called William Wilberforce. William hated slavery but he knew that it wasn't against the law. He knew that the only way to change the law was to tell important people in Parliament, in London, about slavery.

William Wilberforce became a Member of Parliament and began to make speeches about slavery to the other important people in the land. He told them how cruel it was and that it should be stopped. Some people disagreed and made speeches supporting slavery. They said the slave owners would lose money.

But William continued to talk to people and explain that all people should be free. William was a Christian and he knew that the Bible teaches that cruelty is wrong. People began to listen to him more and more. Ordinary people talked about slavery and whether it should be stopped. Soon, William had enough supporters and there was a vote in Parliament to stop slavery. William's side won!

Of course, Britain couldn't stop all of the slavery in the world, but soon other countries also passed new laws to stop the buying and selling of slaves. Eventually, Africans were no longer captured and taken away in ships and made to work in strange lands.

The chains around the necks of the slaves were unlocked. Keys were used, but it was talking that really set the slaves free – talking and arguing and speeches by brave, good people like William Wilberforce.

Maybe you have discussions in your classroom? These are your chances to speak about something you think is important – so try to join in.

INTERACTIVE FOLLOW UP ACTIVITIES

Questions
1) Why were African people captured and taken away from their homes a long time ago?
   (They were taken to become slaves.)
2) Where were the slaves taken?
   (Across the seas to work in other countries like America.)
3) How did William Wilberforce help to stop slavery?
   (By telling other people how bad it was, by talking in Parliament, by campaigning.)

Finish off these sentences about slavery by calling out the last word:
* Many African people were forced to become slaves a long time _____ . *(ago)*
* They were captured and tied up with _____ . *(chains)*
* The slaves were forced to work very _____ . *(hard)*
* One man who tried to stop slavery was called William _____ . *(Wilberforce)*
* William didn't stop slavery by fighting, he stopped it by _____ . *(talking)*

What can we learn from this story?
We have learnt about slavery, but what have we learnt about speaking?
(That speaking/talking can change things as much as force.)

NON-INTERACTIVE FOLLOW UP

Summary of the story
- 200 years ago, ordinary people from Africa were captured.
- They were chained up and taken away to become slaves.
- They were packed into ships, taken across the world then bought and sold.
- Slaves had no freedom – they were owned by white people and often treated very cruelly.
- Slaves had to work hard but were paid no money.
- A man called William Wilberforce helped to end slavery by telling people in Parliament how cruel and wrong it was.
- He changed the world by speaking, arguing thoughtfully and telling people about others.

Reflection
It is good that slavery has ended but there are still many things wrong in the world. Be like William Wilberforce and speak up for what you believe in and don't be afraid to say something to help other people.

Prayer
Lord God, thank you that slavery is now against the law and that people are no longer taken away in chains like they were. Please help us to remember brave William Wilberforce and to learn that speaking up can change what is wrong. Amen.

2c Recognising Choices

Objective
To help children recognise the choices they can make and the differences between right and wrong.

PSHE/Citizenship links
2c (Recognising choices)

Props
(Not essential): a wallet or purse – preferably with some notes in, which could be produced at an appropriate time in the story.

Introduction
It's nice to have choices. Having choices means that you can choose things. You might be able to choose what you have for your tea tonight; maybe you can choose what TV programme you'd like to watch when you get home; sometimes, if you've worked hard at school all week, your teacher might allow you to choose what activity you'd like to do on a Friday afternoon. But do you know that we can also choose how to behave? Listen to this story about two boys, who had a very important choice to make.

Story: What Shall We Do?

Bill and Jason were walking to school. It was a chilly November morning and they could see their breath when they breathed out. They played at being dragons and roared and breathed dragon 'smoke' at each other as they went. There were white, frosty cobwebs shimmering in the hedges and plants of the front gardens that they passed, and the grass along the sides of the pavements was silver and crispy with frost. Bill was glad that his mum had nagged him about wearing his gloves: Jason's hands looked absolutely frozen!

"Breathe on your hands with your dragon breath," said Bill, when he saw how red and cold his friend's hands were. "That'll warm them up!"

Jason tried that, but soon ran out of puff. "It's no good, I'll have to put them in my pockets," he said. "I'll make sure I remember my gloves tomorrow morning, though!"

"Tell you what," said Bill, "I'll lend you one of mine for today, then we can have one each and we can each put just one hand in our pockets!"

"Oh, thanks Bill!" said Jason, gratefully grabbing the glove that Bill offered him.

The two boys stopped to sort out the gloves and, while Jason was putting his one on, Bill noticed something lying on the path in front of them.

"Hey, Jason, come and look at this!" he said, peering down at a flat leather shape. "What d'you think it is?"

"It looks like a wallet – my dad's got one a bit like it, except his is brown. He keeps all of his cards and his money in it."

"Oh wow!" exclaimed Bill. "Do all wallets have money in, then? I hope this one does!"

Jason picked up the wallet and tried opening it, but his hands were too cold and stiff to manage it. "You try," he said to Bill, who had already taken his one remaining glove off.

29

"Oh *double* wow!!" shouted Bill, dancing up and down in his excitement. "There's LOADS of money in here! Oh brilliant – if we split the money and have half each, we'll both have stacks and stacks!"

"Hang on!" said Jason. "We can't do that – it's not our money!"

"Of course it is!" laughed Bill. "We found it, didn't we?"

"Well... yes," said Jason, sounding a bit unsure. "But it's stealing, isn't it – stealing from the person the wallet belongs to?"

"Don't be so daft!" said Bill. "Stealing is when you decide to nick something from someone and you actually go and *take it away* from them. We haven't done that with this wallet. We just *found* it. It's quite different."

Jason looked very doubtful. The boys had carried on with their journey to school while they were talking and by this time they had reached the school gates. Bill quickly shoved the wallet into his bag and put it right at the bottom, under his packed lunch. Just as he did that, the whistle went, so they scurried across the playground to where their class was lining up.

Mrs Stone had a busy morning planned for them, and the whole class worked hard at their writing and number work. Even though it was very quiet, because everyone was concentrating and working so hard, Jason just couldn't keep his mind on his work. He was very worried about the wallet. He had a really horrible feeling inside. It almost felt as if he was going to be sick, even though he knew he wasn't ill. He was going to have to talk to Bill about it at playtime.

Jason found his friend under the big tree in the playground. "Oh, Bill," he started. "I just don't feel that it's the right thing to do, to keep the money we found. I feel really horrible inside and I think it's because we're doing a very bad thing. I think we should go and tell Mrs Stone all about it, and she can ask the police to give it back to the person who lost it."

"NO WAY!" said Bill, his eyes wide with amazement at what he was hearing. "I've never had the chance of having so much money before and I'm not just going to give it back to someone who was so careless with it. They don't even deserve to have so much money, if they can't look after it!"

"Well, I still think it's wrong and that it's stealing," replied Jason. "I don't want any of the money, because it doesn't belong to me. If I were you, I would take it straight to Mrs Stone and let her deal with it." He walked away very sadly, because he'd never argued with Bill before.

After play, the class did lots more work. Jason still couldn't concentrate and kept looking over at Bill. Funnily enough, Bill didn't seem to be working like he usually did, either. In fact, he was beginning to look a bit uncomfortable. Each time Jason looked at him, he looked away quickly. At lunchtime, Bill kept right away from Jason and didn't join in with any of the usual games everyone played together.

At the start of the afternoon, Mrs Stone said, "Well, Class 2, you worked so hard and quietly this morning that I'm going to let you choose this afternoon. You can have a free choice of what you want to do for the whole afternoon. Does anyone have any ideas of what they would like to choose?" She looked round and spotted Bill's hand up. "Yes, Bill," she said.

"Well my choice has been very difficult to make, Mrs Stone, but I've decided now," he said, looking a bit fidgety. "I want to tell you about something that Jason and I found on our way to school this morning…" Bill gave Mrs Stone the wallet with all of the money inside and told her all about finding it, while the rest of the class played in the sand, made models and dressed up in the home corner.

The boys walked home from school together, each with one hand in a pocket and the other hand wearing one of Bill's gloves. "Good choice, Bill!" smiled Jason at his friend. "Good choice."

INTERACTIVE FOLLOW UP ACTIVITIES

Questions

1) What was the weather like on that day in the story?
   (Cold and frosty.)
2) Who can remember the boys' names?
   (Bill and Jason.)
3) What did they find on their way to school?
   (A wallet containing lots of money.)

Getting the message

1) What did Jason want to do with the wallet?
   (He wanted to give it to his teacher, so she could give it to the police and it could be returned to its owner.)
2) Which one of these things did Bill want to do with the money at first? Put your hands up when you hear the right one.
   - Bill wanted to give the wallet and the money to his teacher.
   - Bill wanted to keep all the money for himself.
   - Bill wanted to give the wallet to his mum.
   - Bill wanted to share the money out between him and Jason. ✓

Learning more

1) Why is it wrong just to keep things that you find?
   (They don't belong to you; the person who lost them might really need them; they might be really sad that they lost them.)
2) What should you do if you find something that you think someone might have lost?
   (Tell an adult such as your teacher, a dinner lady, your parents or a police officer.)
3) This story is about choices – choosing what to do. What choice did Bill have to make?
   (Whether he was going to tell anyone about the wallet, or whether he was going to keep the money and not say anything.)
4) Give me a thumbs-up if you think Bill made the <u>right</u> choice in the end, or a thumbs-down if you think he chose the <u>wrong</u> thing in the end.

31

NON-INTERACTIVE FOLLOW UP

Summary of the story

- Bill and Jason were walking to school.
- They found a wallet with lots of money in it.
- Bill wanted for him and Jason to share the money and keep it.
- Jason thought that that was stealing and wanted to tell their teacher about it.
- In the end, Bill chose to tell the teacher after all.
- He made a good choice.

Something to think about

1) Is it always easy to make the right choice?
2) Sometimes we have to choose what we know is right, even if it's not what we really want.
3) Look out for times when you can choose to do the right thing.

Reflection

Always try to make the right choice of what to do: if you can choose to be kind or to be nasty, choose to be kind. If you can choose to help someone, or to leave them struggling, choose to help them.

Prayer

Lord God, thank you that we can make choices in our lives. Please help us to make the right choices every day. Teach us what is right and what is wrong, and help us to choose what's right every time, even if it's not always what we want. Amen.

2D AGREEING AND FOLLOWING RULES

Objective
To help children agree and follow rules and understand how rules help them.

PSHE/Citizenship links
2d (Rules)

Props
(Not essential): examples of litter, e.g. empty cans and crisp packets; a large piece of paper with graffiti-type writing etc on

Introduction
School would be so much better if there weren't so many rules! There's so much you're not allowed to do, even though it would be great fun; and there are so many things you have to do, that aren't any fun at all. Just imagine a whole day at school without any rules: wouldn't it be fantastic…? Listen to this story and see what you think.

STORY: RETURN OF THE RULES

One Friday afternoon, Floyd got told off for the third time that day. "Floyd!" said Mrs Collins. "Please do NOT run around the classroom! It's against the rules, you know."

"Aw, I'm fed up with school rules," grumbled Floyd. "It's not fair! We're not allowed to do anything that's fun round here."

"Yeah," said Kim, "school rules are really BORING. We all wish we didn't have them!" Mrs Collins saw that lots of her class nodded and agreed with Kim and Floyd.

On Monday morning, the children in Class 3 lined up in the playground. They waited patiently for the whistle to go before they followed Mrs Collins into the classroom. Floyd pushed in at the front of the line as usual, and everyone waited for Mrs Collins to tell him off and send him to the back, like she did every morning.

But this time, Mrs Collins just turned round and said, "Right Class 3, follow me." Floyd grinned like mad as he led the line of children into the classroom. Everyone else was a bit surprised, because they knew that Mrs Collins was usually so fair and didn't like it when people pushed in. Perhaps she just hadn't noticed.

In the cloakroom, there was the usual pushing and shoving, and Sally's coat got knocked off her peg onto the muddy floor. Steven was in a grumpy mood that morning and when he saw Sally's coat on the floor, he didn't bother to pick it up for her. Instead, he just walked all over it with his mucky shoes. Sally ran into the classroom to tell Mrs Collins.

"Oh well, never mind Sally," said Mrs Collins, when she heard about the coat. Sally just stood there and didn't know what to say next. She started crying, because she was worried what her mum would say about her coat and she thought it wasn't fair that Steven hadn't even got told off.

"Right, children," said Mrs Collins. "Shall we start off this morning by hearing your news from the weekend? Who did something that they'd like to tell us about?"

33

Now, that was the moment that Asif had been waiting for. He'd been away for the weekend with his family and was bursting to tell the class all about it. His hand shot up and Mrs Collins asked him to tell everyone about his camping trip.

"Well, we went camping and..." started Asif, but had to stop because Jamil and Shona, who were sitting at the back of the carpet area, had started to argue quite loudly. In fact they even started to fight. Usually Mrs Collins would have stopped them straight away and made them sit as far away from each other as possible, so that Asif could carry on with his talk. But this morning, Mrs Collins just sat there and let them carry on. This was going to be a very strange day indeed.

As the morning went on, more and more odd things happened. When it was time for doing number work, Gary and Louise started throwing plastic cubes at each other. One hit Sharon in the face, but Mrs Collins didn't do anything. At playtime everyone just dashed out of the classroom without waiting to be told and Lucy got squashed in the rush. And outside, things were even worse. Normally when it was wet and muddy, the children weren't allowed on the grass, but today nobody stopped them. All the bigger boys were sliding about in the mud and having a whale of a time.

When the children came in after play, the cloakroom was a sea of mud and because no one told the children to change their shoes, they all wore their outdoor shoes indoors, so the classroom floor was soon horribly muddy. That afternoon, not much work got done. Everyone was being far too noisy and excited, because Mrs Collins just didn't seem to stop them from shouting. Sam got upset because Sarah drew all over his picture of a lighthouse; David decided to draw his own pictures on one of Mrs Collins' beautiful wall displays; Gina and Hollie spent most of the afternoon sliding on the floor of the girls' toilets and giggling, until Hollie fell and hurt her knee.

Suddenly the classroom went quiet. There was mud everywhere, the classroom was a mess, Hollie was crying because her knee hurt, Sam was still upset about his picture and Sally was worried about her dirty coat. In fact most of the children were wondering what their mums were going to say about the mud they had all over their clothes and shoes.

Mrs Collins stood up. "Now then, children," she said. "Who has enjoyed today?"

Floyd spoke up, "At first it was BRILLIANT! We could all do just what we wanted," he said, "but..."

"But," said Sam. "It all went a bit wrong and it stopped being so brilliant. Now I just want to go home and I'd like it to be just a normal day again tomorrow, please!"

"So, it turns out that the rules we have in school about not rushing about, not playing on the wet grass and working quietly actually make school MORE fun, not less fun, don't they?" said Mrs Collins. "Well, tomorrow we'll go back to our old school rules, I think – so no trying to push in at the front of the line in the morning, Floyd!" she smiled.

Everyone laughed and was very pleased – even Floyd.

INTERACTIVE FOLLOW UP ACTIVITIES

Questions

1) Why did Mrs Collins have a day without any school rules?

   (The children thought it would be more fun not to have any rules in school.)

2) What were some of the bad things that happened that day?

   (People pushed in, Sally's coat got dirty, no-one got told off, people were arguing and fighting, people got hurt, the classroom display and Sam's picture got drawn on, etc.)

3) What did the children decide in the end?

   (School works better and is more fun when there are rules.)

Getting the message

1) What can we learn from this story?

   (School rules are there to help us all be safe and enjoy our day.)

2) Here are four rules. When you hear each one, put your hand up if you think that it would be a good rule for our school and keep your hand down if you think it's a bad rule.

   - Don't run in the classrooms or corridors. Put up your hand if you think that's a good rule. *(Ask a couple of children why they voted the way they did.)*
   - No talking <u>at all</u> in school. Put up your hand if you think that's a good rule. *(Ask a couple of children why they voted the way they did.)*
   - Don't push in front of other people: wait until it's your turn. Put up your hand if you think that's a good rule. *(Ask a couple of children why they voted the way they did.)*
   - No running in the playground. Put up your hand if you think that's a good rule. *(Ask a couple of children why they voted the way they did.)*

Learning more

1) Can you think of some rules that would help us all in school? *(Ask for 4 volunteers to come up and tell everyone their rules, and explain why they think they would be helpful.)*

2) For each of these things, call out "Yes" if it's good for school and "No" if it isn't (no shouting!):

   - pushing
   - shouting
   - waiting your turn
   - not listening
   - helping other people
   - being nasty to someone
   - doing what your teacher says

3) Why do you think we have rules at school?

   (To keep us all safe; to make sure that everyone enjoys their day and doesn't have it spoiled by others.)

Non-interactive Follow Up

Summary of the story

- The children in Class 3 thought that school rules were silly.
- Their teacher, Mrs Collins, gave them a day without rules.
- Lots of boys and girls got hurt and upset, and everyone got very muddy.
- In the end, all the children agreed that school was much better when everyone obeyed the rules.

Something to think about

- Do you think that school rules are a good idea?
- Can you think of 3 school rules that you think are good?
- Can you think of 2 school rules that you might have broken before?

Reflection

If we didn't have any rules, we would be much unhappier. People would get hurt and upset, if we all went round doing exactly what we felt like all the time. Sometimes rules seem like a bit of a nuisance, but just think how bad it would be without them!

Prayer

Lord God, thank you that our school has rules that make it a safe place to be. Please remind us that rules are there to help us, if we ever feel like breaking them. Help us all to keep to the rules that we have in our school, so that we can all enjoy our time together. Amen

2E MEETING NEEDS

Objective

Realising that people and other living things have needs, and that they have responsibilities to meet them.

PSHE/Citizenship links

2e (People's needs)

Props

Picture of Mother Theresa downloaded from the internet *(try clicking the 'images' icon on www.google.co.uk then typing in 'Mother Theresa')*

Introduction

Most of the people we know have somewhere to live, enough food, a school to go to and family or friends to look after them. There are lots of people in the world who don't have any of those things, though. Whose job is it to look after those people, I wonder?

TRUE STORY: SOMEONE NEEDS TO DO SOMETHING!

Theresa was a young Christian nun who worked in India. She was a teacher in a school in Calcutta and all the children in her class loved her, because she was very kind. She loved the school, which was in a handsome building and was full of happy children. She enjoyed walking in the gardens in the cool evenings, because she loved the beautiful flowers and plants that grew there. Theresa had a very good and busy life.

One thing bothered her, though. When she went out of the school on her days off and walked through the streets of Calcutta, she noticed something very sad. Wherever she looked, there seemed to be poor people, with nowhere to go. Many of them looked very hungry and ill; there were children with nobody at all to look after them and most of them seemed to be actually *living* out on the streets: they simply didn't have a home to go to.

She prayed hard and thought, "These poor people really need some help. Isn't there anyone who can do something?" It wasn't long before she realised that she needed to do something to help, herself. She gave up her job at the school she loved so much and learnt how to be a nurse. Then she went to one of the poorest parts of the city and opened a little school. It was a school that you didn't need to pay to go to, so even the poorest children could come. Before long her school was full to bursting.

The trouble was, that the children needed books and pencils to help them with their schoolwork, and also food and medicines, because many of them were hungry and quite poorly. Mother Theresa, as she became known, didn't have enough money to pay for all of these things. It was a big problem.

But gradually, more and more people heard about Theresa's work. They heard how she loved and cared for the poorest people in the city, who no one else seemed to care about. Soon, they started to send money, books, food and medicines to help her in her work. Some of the pupils that she had taught in her first school were grown up now and came along to offer their help too. They became teachers in Mother Theresa's special school.

37

The school grew and grew.

You'd have thought that Mother Theresa would have been very pleased that she was doing so much good for the poor children she taught and cared for, but she was still bothered. Now that she worked in the poorest part of the city, she saw more and more people who were suffering. She noticed that many people suffered from dreadful diseases and had no one to care for them at all.

She decided that what they needed was a hospital where they could come and be looked after properly, so she opened a home in an old church that wasn't used anymore, where very ill people could come and be loved and cared for. They were so grateful to have a comfortable bed, instead of having to lie out on the filthy streets of the city. Even the ones who were so ill that they died, were happy to have somewhere comfortable to spend their last days. Mother Theresa made sure that they all got the best care that they could be given and made them feel loved.

Just like with the school beforehand, more and more people heard about Mother Theresa's hospital. They realised that there were thousands and thousands of homeless, poor people who desperately needed help and unless someone did something, like Theresa had, they would carry on suffering terribly. So people from all over the world started sending money, food and medicines, and also came to work at the hospital in Calcutta.

Now there are hospitals and homes in other cities in India and all over the world that are run by the charity that Mother Theresa started, so people everywhere are being helped.

INTERACTIVE FOLLOW UP ACTIVITIES

Questions
1) What country did Theresa work in?
   (India)
2) Who knows what a nun is?
   (A woman who has given her life to serve and worship God.)
3) Theresa loved her first school, so why was she unhappy?
   (She'd seen the terrible suffering of the poor people of Calcutta.)
4) Did Theresa leave it up to someone else to do something about the poor people?
   (No, she realised that it was up to her to do something.)

Getting the message
1) The first important thing that Mother Theresa did was to notice that the poor people of Calcutta had no one to help them or look after them. What was the next thing that she did?
   (She decided to do something about it herself.)
2) Was Mother Theresa the only person in the story who saw that something needed doing and decided to help?
   (No: the other people who heard about her work and sent money, or came to work with her, did the same.)

Learning more

Mother Theresa gave up her whole life to look after people who had nobody else to care for them. Perhaps one or two of you in this hall today might go on to do something like that one day, but everybody here can be just like Mother Theresa in all sorts of little ways. (*Ask for 4 volunteers to come and pretend to be somebody else.*)

1) (*Child 1: choose a popular child with plenty of friends*) Just imagine that you've often spotted Tracey here looking lonely and sad at school. You've noticed that she doesn't seem to have anyone to play with. What could you do to make her feel better? (*Look out for her at playtimes and invite her to join in your games / invite her to your house to play.*)

2) (*Child 2 & child 3*) Now this might look just like Jonathan, but in fact he's a rabbit called Bugsy. Now Bugsy lives in a hutch in Sally's shed. What are some of the things that Bugsy needs? (*Food, water, straw, etc.*) Can Bugsy get all of these things for himself? (*No!*) So, when Sally sees that he's hungry, thirsty or chilly, what should she do? (*Look after him and provide for his needs.*)

3) (*Child 4*) Oh my! You're looking tired *Sita*! *Sita* is a mum and she's been out at work all day. She's come home, the house is a mess, the children are all watching the telly and arguing and they are hungry. Poor *Sita*! Imagine you are one of *Sita's* children. What could you do for *Sita*? (*Stop arguing / offer to do some tidying up / lay the table / if you were older you could make her a cup of tea / maybe just give her a hug to make her feel loved.*)

NON-INTERACTIVE FOLLOW UP

Summary of the story

- Theresa was a nun who worked at a school in Calcutta, in India.
- She loved her job at the school, but was sad because there were so many poor people on the streets of the city with no one to care for them.
- She decided to do something to help them and opened a small school of her own.
- People from far and wide heard about how she cared for the poor children and began to send money to help her.
- She began opening more schools, hospitals and homes and made everyone feel welcome and loved.
- Her ideas have spread across the world and now hundreds of people help her charity by sending money or by going to work in the hospitals and homes themselves.

Something to think about

1) Someone in your class is in trouble because they've lost their reading book. They need help. What could you do?

2) It's a cold day out on the playground and the dinner lady looks fed up with children who are arguing. What could you do to cheer her up?

Reflection

Every person and even every animal has needs. We all need to be cared for in some way. Look out at school and at home for ways of being kind to people who need help. Sometimes all they need is a friendly word or a smile.

Prayer

Lord God, thank you for people like Mother Theresa. Please help me to notice when people around me need help. Help me make a difference to people's lives in small ways every day. Amen.

2F BELONGING TO GROUPS AND COMMUNITIES

Objective
To help children understand that they belong to various groups and communities.

PSHE/Citizenship links
2f (Belonging)

Preparation
This assembly is in the form of a short play script and requires three volunteer children to read parts B, C and D at the front. The ideal volunteers would be three confident, good readers from Y2 with strong clear voices – any mixture of boys and girls. A short practice before the assembly would be very helpful and each child will need a copy of the script. The teacher reads part A.

Prop
£5 note

Introduction
Today's assembly is about belonging. My shoes belong to me. This book belongs to the school. The piano belongs in the hall. This five pound note belongs to a friend of mine – I'd better pay it back. But what about you – where do you belong? Let's think about that, with the help of three actors.

PLAY: BELONGING

A Right, we have three new children here today – they've just come to this school – which class do you belong to?

B I belong to Class 3.

C I belong to Class 2.

D I'm in Class 2 too.

A I didn't know we had a class two-two! Well, anyway, now you all belong to this school.

B My brother belongs to the school football team here.

C My sister belongs to the netball team.

D I belong to the beginners' recorder club.

A That's great – did you belong to any groups at your last schools?

B I went to sewing club at lunchtimes.

C I was in the after-school art group.

D I belonged to the choir.

A Amazing – so many things to belong to – what about at home?

B I belong to my mum and dad!

C I belong to my family, with my brothers and sisters.

D I belong to my wider family in a way too – my aunts and uncles, cousins and grandparents.

A And do you know any other groups outside school you can belong to?

B My friend is in the Brownies.

C My brother has joined the Cubs.

D I'd like to belong to the local gym club when I'm a bit older.

A Are there any more?

B You can belong to the RSPCA if you're interested in animals.

C I'm a member of the Dennis the Menace Fan Club.

D Cool – I'd like to belong to that!

A Some people belong to a church or a religious group, which is very important to them.

B My next-door neighbour goes to the Roman Catholic Church every week.

C My friend Jamila belongs to the Sikh faith.

D Some people who belong to the Jewish faith wear special clothes – I've seen them.

A There are lots and lots of things to belong to – we all belong to the neighbourhood where we live as well.

B We all belong to our local town or village or city.

C We all belong to Europe.

D And everyone belongs to the world – we're all sharing the same planet.

A Do you think it's important to belong to something?

B Yes, of course – we would be lonely if we didn't.

C And bored.

D Belonging to a group of people makes you feel special.

A I agree – I'm glad that all of us belong in this school.

INTERACTIVE FOLLOW UP ACTIVITIES

Questions

1) What does everyone here belong to?

   (The school.)

2) What else did the children belong to?

   (Families, clubs, etc.)

3) Why did the children think that belonging to something was important?

   (So you don't get bored or lonely; it makes them feel special.)

Clubs

- Hands up who belongs to something like a club out of school *(ask children to say which club/group).*

- Hands up who would like to belong to something when they are older.

Show of hands

Put your hand up if you belong to one of these:

- Sports club
- School club or group
- A church
- A fan club
- A class in this school

NON-INTERACTIVE FOLLOW UP

Summary of the play script
- The three children talked about the things they belonged to.
- They belonged to the school, to their class and to their families.
- Some of them belonged to clubs too, like sports clubs.
- There are also churches and faith groups that people belong to.
- In the end they noticed that everyone belongs to the world – our planet Earth.

Something to think about
1) Belonging to different groups is good – perhaps you could join something.
2) You can always go along and see what it's like.
3) A lot of the trouble in the world is caused by people who don't understand the groups that others belong to – so let's try to find out about them.

Reflection
Think about all of the groups you belong to, at home and at school. Think about joining new groups and taking part – it's good to belong. And be kind to those who don't belong.

Prayer
Lord God, thank you that we all belong to this school and to many other groups and clubs. Thank you for our families and friends and classmates. Help us to be kind to other people who don't belong, especially lonely children that we see. Amen.

2g Improving the Environment

Objective
To help children understand what improves and harms their local, natural and built environments and about some of the ways people look after them.

PSHE/Citizenship links
2g (Environments), 2b (Taking part in debates)

Props
(Not essential): examples of litter, e.g. empty cans and crisp packets

Introduction
Everything needs to be taken care of: people, pets, gardens, books, cars and even roads and buildings. Today's story is about a class who went on a short visit and found a place that needed taking care of *(hold up the litter).*

Story: A Walk in the Park

"Right Class 2, please go and put your coats on and line up by the door." Rasmeet and Kieron rushed towards the coat pegs hoping that Mrs Barnard, their teacher, wouldn't see them.

"Rasmeet, Kieron – be careful or you'll knock someone over!" But the friends were too excited to worry about being told off today, because they were all going to the park.

Mrs Barnard counted the pairs of children when they were lined up.

"Thirty-three – good that's everybody. Right, just before we set off children, who can remind me why we are walking to the park today?" Rasmeet put up her hand, along with half the class. Mrs Barnard asked another girl. "Yes, Pippa?"

"We're going to look at good things and bad things."

"That's right, good girl; we're going to look at good things people have done to the park recently and bad things people have done to the park recently." Rasmeet still had her hand in the air. "Yes, Rasmeet?"

"You want us to find three improvements."

"That's an excellent word – well done. Yes, see if you can all spot three improvements (that's things that have made the park better) *and* three things that make the park worse." Mrs Barnard then gave them another reminder about road safety and they set off, along with two parent helpers.

It wasn't far to the park, just down Chestnut Avenue, past the shops and across the main road at the traffic lights. As soon as they were through the park gate, Kieron started bouncing up and down with excitement.

"Mrs Barnard – will we be allowed to go on the swings and slides?"

"I hope so Kieron, later on, but first I want to see how good you are at spotting the good and bad changes." He looked around – there was certainly a lot to see:
- There were people walking with prams and pushchairs.
- There were three or four dogs being exercised.

43

- There were two people playing with a frisbee on the grass.
- There were trees and paths and bushes and... *the pond*.

There were always ducks at the pond, but today there was something else in there – a supermarket trolley had been pushed into the water. It was lying on its side with two muddy wheels sticking into the air.

Rasmeet had noticed lots of things too.

- There were two men, from the Council she guessed, who were planting trees by the car park.
- There were crisp bags and fish and chip wrappers blowing around by the toddlers' climbing frame.
- There were four tennis courts and a bowling green.
- There was the brick building where the toilets were – it was covered in spray-painted writing, called 'graffiti'.
- There were the swings for the older children and next to them a brand new shiny metal slide.

"Hey cool – look Kieron," said Rasmeet, but Kieron was looking the other way and pointing to the old railings which had just been painted bright blue. There was a lot to see when you really started looking, he thought.

After a few more minutes walking, Mrs Barnard stopped everybody and asked the class to gather round. She asked if anybody had spotted any good changes to the park. Everyone put their hand up – there were lots. Then she asked about things that made the park a worse place. Again, everybody in the class put up their hand and there was a long list.

"Well that's wonderful Class 2," said Mrs Barnard. "I think you definitely deserve to have some time on the play equipment." A few moments later, Kieron was shooting down the new slide and Rasmeet was at the top of the huge wooden climbing frame, along with most of her classmates. They rushed around trying all of the equipment and showing off noisily. It had been a great morning. Then Mrs Barnard called out that it was time to go back to school and told everyone to line up.

"Aww can't we have just five more minutes here?" said Kieron.

"I'm sorry," said Mrs Barnard, "we need to go now or we'll be late for lunch."

"What are we going to do this afternoon, Mrs Barnard?" said Rasmeet.

"Well, first of all we're going to talk about the good and bad things in the park and then draw some of them – I hope you can remember what they are."

Rasmeet and Kieron could remember quite a few - can you?

INTERACTIVE FOLLOW UP ACTIVITIES

Questions

1) What were some of the good things that people had done to the park?

    (E.g. new slide, trees planted, railings painted.)

2) What were some of the bad things that people had done to the park?

    (E.g. graffiti, supermarket trolley in the pond, litter.)

3) What things could be done in the park to make it a better place for everyone?

    (Employing people to clean graffiti and litter, and the pond; have a park keeper to watch over it; more and better facilities, etc.)

Getting the message

1) What can we learn from this story?

    (We need to look after places like parks or they will be spoiled.)

2) The children in Mrs Barnard's class said 4 things about the park that afternoon when they got back to school.

    • Someone said, "No-one looks after the park." Put up your hand if you agree with that.

    • Someone said, "It's best if everyone helps look after the park." Put up your hand if you agree with that.

    • Someone said, "Planting trees improves the park." Put up your hand if you agree with that.

    • Someone said, "Litter doesn't really spoil the park." Put up your hand if you agree with that.

Learning more

1) How wildlife is affected: ask for 4 volunteers to come out and help explain about polluting the pond. Tell the children that you're going to show how the supermarket trolley can affect the animals in the park.

    i)   What happens if a metal trolley is left in water, in the pond? *It goes rusty. (Child 1 mimes pushing a shopping trolley.)*

    ii) What creatures are harmed by the rusty water? *Frogs and fish and insects. (Child 2 mimes being a frog, Child 3 a fish with open mouth.)*

    iii) If all the fish, insects and plants die, which creatures will have less food? *Ducks and other birds. (Child 4 pretends to be a bird.)*

    iv) Run through the sequence again with miming. Explain that this is an example of pollution.

2) For each of these things, call out "Yes" if it's good for the park and "No" if it isn't *(no shouting)*:

    • litter
    • graffiti
    • flowers
    • new play equipment
    • broken glass
    • trees
    • football pitches
    • noisy traffic

3) Name some things that can make a park good for older people.

    (E.g. seats, quiet areas, shelters, gardens, animals, walks, wheelchair access, scenic views, information boards, places for dogs to exercise, etc.)

NON-INTERACTIVE FOLLOW UP

Summary of the story

* Rasmeet and Kieron and the rest of Class 2 went to visit the local park.
* Their teacher, Mrs Barnard, asked them to look out for good and bad things that people had done to the park.
* They found 3 good things: new trees, a new slide and railings, which had been painted.
* They also found 3 bad things: litter, graffiti and a supermarket trolley polluting the pond.

Something to think about

1) How can you help to look after the places around you?
2) What can you do about litter?
3) Watch out for the changes in local places and notice who is making them.

Reflection

Look after the places around you – your environment. Say thank you to those people who work to make our environment better. Help to care for the world so that it's a better place for everyone to live in.

Prayer

Lord God, thank you for parks and playgrounds, and places where there are animals and beautiful trees and flowers. And thank you for all the people who look after important buildings like schools, homes, offices and shops. Please help me to take care of places in my local area. Amen.

2h Making a Contribution

Objective
To help children appreciate how different people can make different kinds of contributions to the life of a class or school.

PSHE/Citizenship links
2h (Contributing to the life of the class or school)

Props
(Not essential): a branch of a tree or bush

Introduction
Do you know anything about beavers? Beavers are animals which spend most of their time in water. They are amazing builders and they can cut down trees with their teeth to build their homes. They depend on trees for food too – because they eat the bark from the branches. Beavers also depend on each other, as we'll find out from this story.

Story: Arnold's Contribution

Crash! Another tall thin birch tree toppled over and came smashing to the ground. All around the edge of the lake there were beavers chewing away at the smaller trees, cutting through the wood with their amazing strong, yellow teeth. As soon as a tree fell to the ground, the beaver that had gnawed through its trunk would start to chew off the branches and drag them into the water nearby.

"Arnold – why aren't you cutting down any trees?" said a large brown beaver to a smaller beaver, who was standing by the edge of the lake.

"I'm really no good at biting through big tree trunks – I can do the smaller branches but I just can't get the hang of these big ones."

"But Arnold, every beaver in this community needs to cut down trees or we won't be able to build a dam. And if we don't build a dam then this lake won't be deep enough for us to build a lodge to live in during the winter – every beaver knows that." The big beaver disappeared, dragging a long black branch towards the new dam which the beavers were making, at the edge of the lake.

Of course Arnold knew this. He was only young, but the same thing had happened to him every year. Each spring all the beavers in the lake community would start to talk about the new dam and where to build it. Then they would choose the best trees to cut down with their teeth, and they would drag the branches to the edge of the lake and pile them up to make a dam, adding stones and mud to stop the water getting through.

And every spring, Arnold tried to join in with the dam building. He tried to cut down trees. He tried to drag heavy branches. He tried to collect mud and stones. But, truth be told, he was just no good at these things. And so Arnold used to sit at the edge of the lake and watch the other beavers hard at work. And all of them would nag at him and complain that he wasn't helping and tell him to get to work. And Arnold would always reply, "But I'm no good at cutting down trees."

47

The same thing happened in the autumn too. That was when the beavers built their special home called a 'lodge'. When the dam was finished, the lake would fill up with water, getting deeper and deeper. By autumn, it would be ready for the beavers to make a little island of mud in the middle. They would pile sticks on the little island and hollow out a space in the centre, where they would live during the winter. It was a wonderful place to live because it had secret underwater entrances to keep away the beavers' enemies like wolves and it also kept them warm in the freezing winter months.

But Arnold was no good at building lodges either.

"Come on Arnold – get some sticks for the lodge!" the big, busy beavers would call to him in the autumn. "Or we'll never finish before winter."

Arnold did try to help. He could collect sticks but he didn't like doing it because he always put them in the wrong place or he picked up the wrong type of branch. Then the other beavers would moan at him again.

"What are we going to do with you, Arnold?" they would say. "Every beaver needs to make a contribution to the community you know."

And Arnold would reply, "But I do make a contribution – just not building. I make a different kind of contribution."

"Oh yes, Arnold, and what's that?" they would reply.

"I cheer everyone up and I make other beavers laugh," said Arnold.

"Well, that's very nice, but cheering people up doesn't build a home for the winter does it? You need to make a proper contribution Arnold."

And this made Arnold a little bit miserable, although he knew his time would come.

And Arnold's time did come. Soon the lodge was finished and winter arrived. The lake's water became icy and snow covered the mountains all around. The plants and trees stopped growing and there was no fresh food to eat. The beaver community stayed inside the lodge, warm and safe.

But as the winter months dragged on, it became even darker and colder. The beavers became bored and weary. The only food they had to eat were the green branches they had stored under water in the summer. They tasted sour and slimy. Everyone in the beaver community was fed up.

Well, everyone except one. Arnold was not fed up. He liked the winter months in the lodge because he had an audience.

"Hey, Arnold – how about cheering us up?" said one of the big beavers. "You said that's what you like to do."

And that's exactly what Arnold did.

First, he told the other beavers all about the time he tried to cut down his first tree. It took him six days to chew through the trunk and when he finally got through it he forgot to make sure it fell away from him. The tree landed right on top of his tail pinning him to the ground for hours. Luckily, two other beavers heard him wailing with fright and chewed the branches off his tail.

And then there was the time that he accidentally filled in the entrance to the lodge. He thought it was a hole and plugged it up with sticks. The poor beavers inside couldn't get out for ages.

The big beavers roared with laughter at Arnold's tales of building disasters. Then Arnold told them jokes all about silly wolves and nutty owls and crazy beavers from other lakes, who were even worse builders than he was. Then Arnold sang some funny songs he'd made up. The audience of beavers chuckled and cackled and giggled for ages.

"Oh Arnold, you're so funny!" they said. "You've really cheered us up." And so the winter months in the lodge were not so miserable for the beavers any more. Every day, Arnold entertained the others with his tales and jokes and songs. And because they enjoyed it so much, he tried new things too – impressions of the older beavers, silly walks and funny rhymes. The beavers loved Arnold's antics.

"I think I've made a contribution to the community now," he said.

"You certainly have, Arnold, you certainly have."

INTERACTIVE FOLLOW UP ACTIVITIES

Questions

1) What was Arnold good at?
   (Cheering up and entertaining the other beavers.)
2) Why did some beavers complain about him?
   (Because he didn't help with the building.)
3) Why did the beavers build a dam and a lodge?
   (The dam was to make the lake deeper and the lodge was to live in, safe from predators.)

Put your thumb up if I say something true about this story:

- Arnold did try to help with the building. *(T)*
- Arnold wasn't very good at building. *(T)*
- Arnold didn't make a contribution to the beavers' community. *(F)*
- The beavers needed cheering up in winter. *(T)*
- Arnold's contribution wasn't important. *(F)*

What can we learn from this story?

We can learn that different people contribute to a community in different ways. Our school is also a community and it is good when we contribute to it by joining in things.

NON-INTERACTIVE FOLLOW UP

Summary of the story
- A community of beavers were building a dam and a lodge in a lake.
- The beavers cut down trees with their teeth.
- They dragged the branches into the water to make the dam and lodge.
- Arnold didn't help with the building because he wasn't very good at it.
- Some of the beavers complained that Arnold wasn't making a contribution to the community.
- In winter the beavers stayed in the lodge most of the time.
- When the beavers were cold and bored, Arnold cheered them up with jokes and funny stories.
- The beavers agreed that Arnold had made a good contribution.

Something to think about
1) Remember that people, like beavers, can't be good at everything.
2) Cheering people up is a valuable thing to do.

Reflection
Different people are good at different things and it's good when we all make a contribution to our class and our school in different ways. Try to value everyone's contribution.

Prayer
Lord God, thank you that we are all different and that we can all make a contribution to our school community in different ways. Help us to cheer each other up just like Arnold. Amen.

21 Where Money Comes From and Goes To

Objective

To help children to realise that money comes from different sources and can be used for different purposes.

PSHE/Citizenship links

2i (Sources and uses of money)

Props

(Not essential): a used £5 note

Introduction

There is a saying that 'money makes the world go round'. I wonder what that means? Well listen to today's assembly story and you might just get a clue.

Story: The Adventures of a Five Pound Note

"Happy birthday Jamila! How does it feel to be six years old?" Jamila's mum gave her a big hug.

"It feels just the same as when I was five," said Jamila.

"Well, never mind – you come and open your birthday cards – a whole pile of them came with the post today."

Jamila loved opening cards. There were pictures of animals, flowers, sparkly girls, fairies, cartoons and lots more. There were cards from friends, aunts, uncles, grandparents and neighbours. But the best card was from Jamila's great grandma because there was something inside – a five pound note.

"Oh look Mum!" said Jamila. "Can I buy a beanie with this?"

"Of course you can – we'll go to the shops on Saturday." And that's just what they did. Jamila walked into town with her mum and went to her favourite toy shop. She chose a beanie rabbit for her collection and paid for it with the five pound note. There was just a penny change. After shopping with her mum, Jamila went home to play with her new beanie. But what happened to the five pound note?

Well, let's find out. First, it went into the till at the toy shop and there it stayed until half past five when the shop closed. The owner, Mrs Richards, then opened the till, to count all the money. She put the five pound note onto a pile with all the others and then put them into a bag. On Monday morning, Mrs Richards took the bag of money to her local bank where she handed it over to go into her bank account.

At the bank, the lady behind the counter counted the money and wrote down that it needed to be added to Mrs Richards' account. But the five pound note didn't stay at the bank for very long. It was soon put into a metal drawer behind the counter with hundreds of other five pound notes. At two o'clock an elderly gentleman called Mr Stock called into the bank. This was where he kept all his money. He asked to take out £35. The young cashier at the counter gave him three £10 notes and the £5 note which had once belonged to Jamila.

51

So, what happened to it next? Well, Mr Stock needed to pay his gas bill at the post office. He walked down the road and paid the bill using the money he'd been given at the bank. He handed over the five pound note. It was kept at the post office for a day until it was given to a teenage girl called Ella. Ella went to the post office to buy some stamps. She paid with a £20 note and the £5 note was given to her as part of her change.

Ella took the five pound note home and lent it to her brother, Peter. Peter needed it for dinner money at school and the next day he handed it over to the school secretary. That afternoon, the school secretary paid it in at another bank in the town.

The five pound note was kept at the bank for a few days until it was given to a woman called Mrs Nairu. Mrs Nairu withdrew £100 from the bank altogether. The five pound note stayed in Mrs Nairu's purse for a week until she went to church. At the church there was a collection plate for money and Mrs Nairu took the five pound note out of her purse and put it into the plate.

One of the leaders of the church, called Bill, counted the money in the plate and paid it into the bank the following day – it was back at the same bank that Mrs Richards, the toy shop owner, had taken it to!

As before, it didn't stay at the bank for long. It was given to a man called Mr Yates who gave it to a window cleaner called Graham as payment for cleaning the windows of his house. Graham put it in his pocket, but unfortunately he dropped it as he was walking to his van.

The five pound note was picked up off the pavement by an elderly lady called Mrs Porter. She thought about handing it in to the police but decided to keep it instead – she didn't have much money. Mrs Porter put the money under the mattress of her bed where she kept her savings. The five pound stayed under Mrs Porter's bed for 8 years! Then sadly, Mrs Porter became too old to look after herself and had to go into a nursing home. But she hadn't forgotten about the money under her mattress – she gave it to her daughter, including the five pound note.

Mrs Porter's daughter was called Mrs Hutchinson. She had a grandson called Ben and it was Ben's sixth birthday the following Friday. She bought him a card and popped the five pound note inside.

Two days later, a little boy opened a card on his birthday. He whooped with delight when he saw the £5 note inside. It was old and crumpled and tired-looking, but it was his.

I wonder what happened to it next?

INTERACTIVE FOLLOW UP ACTIVITIES

Questions
1) Who can remember some of the things that happened to the five pound note?
   (It was spent on a beanie, put in a bank, used for change, saved, paid to someone, etc.)
2) Who was given the five pound note first?
   (Jamila)
3) What do you think happened to the five pound note next?
   (Open ended.)

Getting the message

1) Is money only used for spending?

    (No, it can be used for lots of things, e.g. saving, giving away, lending, etc.)

2) Which of these things happened to the five pound note in the story? Put up your hand when you think I say something that did happen to it.

    *   It was given as a present. ✓
    *   It was kept in a money box.
    *   It was spent in a shop. ✓
    *   It was used to pay a bill. ✓
    *   It was torn up.
    *   It was saved. ✓
    *   It was lent to someone. ✓
    *   It was kept in a bank. ✓
    *   It was donated to charity. *(Although it was given as a donation in church.)*
    *   It was used to pay someone's wages.

Learning more

1) Where does money come from?

    (Bank notes and coins are made by the Bank of England and the Royal Mint, which are controlled by the government. Banks are given new money in exchange for old and people and shops etc then get new notes and coins from banks.)

2) Why is money important? *(Open ended.)*

NON-INTERACTIVE FOLLOW UP

Summary of the Story

*   Jamila was given a five pound note on her sixth birthday.
*   She bought a beanie rabbit with it at a shop.
*   The shop owner took the five pound note to a bank.
*   Lots of other people used the five pound note.
*   It was spent, saved, given away, lent and finally given as another birthday present.

Something to think about

1) Is it best to spend money or to save it?
2) Does money ever cause people problems?

Reflection

We all like receiving money and spending money, but remember that money can also be saved up for the future and it can be given away. Remember to support charities that need money to help other people.

Prayer

Lord God, thank you for money and for all the ways in which we can spend it. Please help us to be wise with our money and to try to save some of it for the future. Help us also to remember to give money to charities that need it to help other people. Amen.

3A IMPROVING HEALTH

Objective
To help children make simple choices to improve their health.

PSHE/Citizenship links
3a (Improving health)

Props
(Not essential): a bar of soap

Introduction
The world is full of mess and dirt: dust, soil, stains, ink, food leftovers and germs. We're very fortunate because we can easily wash these things off our clothes and our bodies. But just imagine what it would be like if you were in a place where there was no clean water and no soap, and you had to wear the same clothes all the time. And worst of all, what if you were locked up too. Today's story is about people who this happened to and about a brave woman who helped them.

TRUE STORY: ELIZABETH FRY

Elizabeth Fry lived a long time ago, even before your great-great-grandparents were born. When Elizabeth grew up she wanted to become a preacher in church. She did this, but she also wanted to help poor people and those in need. Elizabeth wasn't rich, but she helped them as much as she could.

Then, one day, Elizabeth went somewhere that changed her life. She visited Newgate Prison in London. In those days, all sorts of people went to prison, not just criminals. Elizabeth was shocked to see that the prison was full of poor people, including lots of women and children. They had done nothing wrong, but were locked away all the same.

But what really shocked Elizabeth was how terrible the conditions in the prison were: it was cold, dirty, damp, dark, overcrowded and smelly. The people, including young children, were pale, weak and hungry, and many of them were poorly too. It really was a terrible place. And to make things worse, the prisoners were all mixed together, young and old, men and women – dangerous criminals were put together with innocent people.

Elizabeth realised that nobody really cared for people in prisons – they were locked away out of sight, but something needed to be done. Elizabeth began to tell people she met what it was like in prison – she told ordinary people and she told important people too. Many began to take notice of her.

Elizabeth started to make plans. She thought that people in prison should be able to learn things, so that when they came out they could find work and improve themselves. Soon, because of Elizabeth's efforts, things began to change. New laws were made and prisoners were separated – men and women in different buildings, and dangerous criminals kept apart from children and the poor. Prisons also became cleaner and less dangerous.

Elizabeth started to travel around the country to inspect prisons to check if things really had changed. She also checked mental hospitals and everywhere she went she raised money to buy things like books for the prisoners. As well as this, she encouraged people to become nurses to care for the sick. She did this for 20 years.

Because of the wonderful work of Elizabeth Fry, the prisons in Britain became much better and people in other countries asked Elizabeth to help them improve their prisons too. She visited every prison in France and went round Belgium, Holland, Switzerland and many other countries giving advice. People all over Europe lived much healthier lives because of one woman's work.

Of course children today aren't sent to prison like they were in Elizabeth Fry's time, but they still need to look after themselves to stay healthy. There are still germs and dirt and mess around. So here are four things you can do to keep yourself healthy:

1. Wash your hands before eating.
2. Brush your teeth carefully twice a day.
3. Eat lots of fresh fruit and vegetables.
4. Get some exercise every day – and running around the playground counts as exercise!

INTERACTIVE FOLLOW UP ACTIVITIES

Questions
1) Who did Elizabeth Fry help?
   (People in prisons and the poor.)
2) Why were prisons so terrible?
   (People were crowded together; they were cold, damp, smelly, dirty, etc; prisoners were hungry and bored; poor people were sent to jail.)
3) How did Elizabeth make prisons better?
   (She told people about them and they became cleaner and prisoners were separated.)

Getting the message
1) What can we learn from this story?
   (That people used to live in bad conditions but things are much better today. We need to look after ourselves to stay healthy.)
2) Put your thumb up if I say something that keeps you healthy:
   • Watching TV.
   • Playing sports.
   • Eating lots of pizza, burgers and chips.
   • Having baths and showers, and washing your hair.
   • Eating lots of salads and bread.

Learning more
1) Which foods should you try not to eat lots of if, you want to keep healthy?
   (Fats and sugars.)
2) What activities are good exercise?
   (Open ended.)

NON-INTERACTIVE FOLLOW UP

Summary of the story

- Elizabeth Fry lived a long time ago.
- She was a preacher who liked to help poor people.
- Elizabeth visited a prison in London and saw how terrible it was for people.
- Elizabeth helped to change the laws about prisons and made them much better places.
- She visited other countries and helped them to improve their prisons too.

Reflection

Try to keep yourself clean and healthy. Wash your hands, brush your teeth, exercise and eat good food. Remember those poor people who had to live in dirty prisons who couldn't keep themselves clean and healthy.

Prayer

Lord God, we thank you for Elizabeth Fry and the kind, brave work she did in prisons. Help us to remember those poor people who had to live in terrible, dirty conditions and help me to look after my own body, to keep clean and healthy. Amen.

3B PERSONAL HYGIENE

Objective
To help children understand the importance of maintaining personal hygiene.

PSHE/Citizenship links
3b (Maintaining personal hygiene)

Props
(Optional): a bottle of bubble bath

Introduction
Today's assembly starts with a special kind of long poem called a cautionary verse. A cautionary verse is a funny poem which carries some kind of warning, usually for children. So, let's see if you can work out what this poem is warning you about.

CAUTIONARY VERSE: GRISELDA FUGG, THE GIRL WHO ATE GERMS

This is the tale of Griselda Fugg,
A girl with a grubby face;
She never took a shower or bath,
And caused her family disgrace.

Griselda loved the great outdoors,
The fields, the woods, the park;
She made mud pies and dens in trees
With green and slimy bark.

She kept pet worms and frogs and mice
In boxes, pots and jars;
Along with her collection
Of rusty bits of cars.

Griselda Fugg was never clean,
Her hair was full of knots;
Her hands were always caked with dirt,
And she rarely changed her socks.

Her parents tried their very best,
And told Griselda straight:
"Young lady you must wash at once,
You really look a state."

But Griselda Fugg was naughty;
She stomped around for hours;
"I won't, I won't, I won't!" she cried,
"I can't stand baths and showers!"

Yet her parents didn't argue,
And Griselda got her way;
But as you'll see quite shortly,
She came to regret this day.

But just for now she was happy,
And jumped about with glee,
And rolled across the muddy lawn,
Shouting, "No more washing for me!"

So Griselda gave up cleaning her hands,
And brushing her teeth and hair;
She let her nails grow long and black;
She really didn't care.

So little Miss Griselda Fugg
Grew grubbier by the day,
Until she invited her friend Maxine
To come round to her house to play.

"Err, I'm sorry, I can't Griselda -
I'm already playing with Rose."
"But Maxine, aren't you my best friend?
And why are you holding your nose?"

But Maxine just kind of giggled,
Then turned her back and ran,
Pulling horrible faces,
And using her hand like a fan.

The next day Griselda felt poorly;
She stayed at home in her bed;
The doctor came in and looked at her hands,
And this is what he said.

"Griselda Fugg, no wonder you're sick,
These fingers are covered in germs;
You're spreading bacteria onto your food,
This is the way you get worms."

"Do you like having brown teeth Griselda?
You really don't look very well."
Then the doctor said, "And there's one more thing,
Your feet are beginning to smell."

The next day Griselda felt better;
She got up at quarter to ten,
Then spent two hours in a hot soapy bath,
And never went dirty again.

INTERACTIVE FOLLOW UP ACTIVITIES

Questions

1) Why did Griselda Fugg have a grubby face?

   (She didn't wash.)

2) How did Griselda get dirty?

   (She liked playing outside a lot.)

3) Why did the poem describe Griselda as a naughty girl?

   (She argued with her parents and refused to take a bath or shower.)

4) Why didn't Maxine want to play with Griselda?

   (She was smelly!)

5) How did Griselda become poorly?

   (From bacteria or germs, which got onto her food from her dirty hands.)

Getting the message

1) What can we learn from this story?

   (To keep ourselves clean; to wash our hands, brush our teeth, etc.)

2) Call out the missing words from these sentences.

   • We need to take baths and showers to keep ourselves _____ . (clean)

   • To keep our teeth clean we need to brush them twice a _____ . (day)

   • Before we eat food we should always wash our _____ . (hands)

   • We also need to wash our hair with _____ . (shampoo)

Learning more

1) What are bacteria? Why are they sometimes dangerous?

2) Why is it a good idea to keep your fingernails short?

   (They are easier to clean; bacteria and dirt can get trapped under them.)

NON-INTERACTIVE FOLLOW UP

Summary of the poem

- Griselda Fugg was a girl who didn't like showers or baths.
- She became very dirty especially as she liked playing outdoors.
- Griselda also argued with her parents about washing.
- Her friend Maxine wouldn't play with her because she was starting to smell.
- Griselda became ill and the doctor said it was because bacteria or germs from her dirty hands had got onto her food.
- Griselda realised that she needed to be clean and so had a long bath.

Something to think about

1) Why do we need to keep ourselves clean?
2) Do you brush your teeth and wash your hands really carefully?

Reflection

Keeping yourself clean is good for lots of reasons – you look better and feel better for a start. But don't forget that you can't see bacteria, or germs as we call them, and so you need to wash your hands very carefully before you eat, even if they look clean. Take care of yourself.

Prayer

Lord God, thank you for hot running water, and for baths and showers, which keep us clean. Help us to remember to wash, to brush our teeth well and to take care of our bodies. Amen.

3c How Diseases Spread

Objective
To help children understand how some diseases spread and can be controlled.

PSHE/Citizenship links
3c (How diseases spread)

Props
(Not essential): a packet of tissues

Preparation
This assembly requires the help of a volunteer child, probably from Y2, who is a capable reader. The child (either a girl or boy) needs to play the part of Jo in a mini drama sketch, and so needs to be able to read a script and act a little. Choosing someone in advance and having a practice run through will certainly help. The child will need a copy of the script and will need to be positioned at the front, facing the audience.

Introduction
Today's assembly tells the sad tale of Jo. A little drama sketch will tell you his/her story and _____ is going to play the part of Jo.

PLAY: JO MISSES OUT

Teacher	This is Jo. Jo is very sad. Why are you so sad, Jo?
Jo	Well, it was my birthday last Saturday.
Teacher	Aren't birthdays usually happy?
Jo	Yes, but this one wasn't.
Teacher	What happened?
Jo	Well, I was supposed to be having a party tea with some of my friends and then we were going to go to the cinema.
Teacher	Didn't you go?
Jo	No, I was poorly and had to stay in bed all day.
Teacher	Oh dear, what a rotten birthday – what was the matter with you?
Jo	Mum said I had a virus.
Teacher	Like a cold you mean?
Jo	Yes, it was like a bad cold, but I had a sore throat and a temperature.
Teacher	I see – we all get those sometimes.
Jo	Well it was the worst time for me to be ill.
Teacher	Was the party cancelled then?
Jo	Yes – my dad had to ring all my friends and we didn't go to the cinema.
Teacher	What happened to your party tea?
Jo	I wasn't hungry – but we saved what we could.
Teacher	So, Jo – how did you catch this virus?
Jo	What do you mean?

Teacher	Well, viruses are tiny, tiny things that spread diseases – we usually catch them off other people.
Jo	So is a cold a virus then?
Teacher	Yes, colds are spread by a virus and so are other things like flu, measles, mumps and even diarrhoea.
Jo	I wonder how I caught the virus I had?
Teacher	Were any of your friends poorly last week?
Jo	Erm... well Paul didn't feel very well on Thursday when I played round at his house.
Teacher	What was up with him?
Jo	I think he just had a runny nose – I remember he kept sneezing everywhere.
Teacher	Oh right. Did he use a tissue? *(Hold up tissues.)*
Jo	I can't remember, err, no, I don't think he did.
Teacher	What were you playing?
Jo	We were just playing with Paul's *Gameboy*.
Teacher	It sounds to me like you caught the virus off Paul.
Jo	But how?
Teacher	Well, when a person sneezes, tiny droplets of water fly into the air. A virus could be in those little droplets and if they land on you, you can catch the virus.
Jo	So using a tissue when you sneeze can stop that?
Teacher	Yes – it's the same with coughs – you should cover your mouth and turn away from other people when you sneeze or cough.
Jo	Is that the only way that viruses spread?
Teacher	No, you can catch them by touch too – maybe Paul sneezed on his hand, used the Gameboy, then passed it to you.
Jo	He should have washed his hands then.
Teacher	Quite right – you should too – washing hands is a good way to stop viruses spreading.
Jo	I'll be more careful next time – I don't want to miss another birthday treat.
Teacher	I'm not surprised.

62

INTERACTIVE FOLLOW UP ACTIVITIES

Questions

1) Why did Jo miss a birthday treat?
   (He/she had a virus and was poorly.)
2) How did Jo catch the virus?
   (From Paul – either by him sneezing or touching something which Jo then touched.)
3) How can you stop viruses spreading?
   (By staying away from people who have them, by coughing and sneezing into a tissue or away from other people, by washing your hands.)

Put your hands on your head if I say something about viruses that is true:

- Coughs and sneezes spread diseases. *(T)*
- Colds and flu are spread by viruses. *(T)*
- You should never touch anyone in case you catch a disease. *(F)*
- Putting your fingers or thumb into your mouth can spread diseases. *(T)*
- Most viruses are very dangerous. *(F)*

What can we learn from this story?

Repeat the rhyme (from World War II): *Coughs and sneezes spread diseases.*

NON-INTERACTIVE FOLLOW UP

Summary of the play

- Jo was poorly and missed his/her birthday tea and cinema trip.
- Jo had a virus with a temperature and sore throat, and had to stay in bed.
- It turned out that Jo had caught the virus from Paul.
- Jo found out that viruses can be passed on by coughs and sneezes.
- Viruses can also be passed on by touching things.
- Jo learnt that using tissues or a hanky when you cough or sneeze, and washing your hands, can stop viruses spreading.

Something to think about

1) If you have a cold, make sure you have a hanky or tissues and wash your hands a lot.
2) Try not to cough or sneeze near people or food.

Reflection

Don't worry about viruses – most of them only give you a runny nose or a cough, but do try not to pass them on to other people. Be kind to people who are feeling rotten with colds and sore throats, especially your family.

Prayer

Lord God, help us not to spread viruses by being careful and washing our hands. Thank you that we have medicines to make us better when we catch diseases and please keep us healthy and strong. Amen.

3D GROWING FROM YOUNG TO OLD

Objective
To help children become aware of how people's needs change as they grow from young to old.

PSHE/Citizenship links
3d (Growing older)

Props
A teddy bear, a *Gameboy* or a mobile phone, a clipboard and a walking stick (could be a meter ruler). Ask for 4 sensible Y2 volunteers who enjoy acting before the assembly starts. These children (2 boys 2 girls for preference, but not essential) will represent different ages. Ask them to act out the type of people you will describe (e.g. the baby will crawl and have a teddy; the teenager will play on his *Gameboy* or talk on his mobile phone; the adult will have an important looking clipboard and 'work'; the elderly person will walk slowly with the aid of a stick).

Introduction
Think of all the different sorts of people you know. There will be people of different colours, people with different interests and people of different ages. Today we're going to think about people of different ages and how we change, as we get older.

RIDDLE: HOW MANY LEGS?

Please can I have my four volunteers up here at the front? *(4 children come to front.)* Here are four people I'd like you to meet.

(Pointing to child one.) This is baby Lottie. She gets about by crawling on the floor, because she can't walk yet. She needs help with almost everything. The things that she does best are dribbling, gurgling and crying! Luckily she sleeps a lot. Her favourite toy is her teddy. *(Give teddy to child one, who crawls and then sits and hugs her teddy.)*

(Pointing to child two.) Here's her big brother Grant. He's a teenager and he has to work hard at school. He doesn't do dribbling, gurgling and crying like he used to when he was a baby like Lottie. He spends quite a bit of time talking to his friends on his mobile phone / playing on his Gameboy in the evenings. *(Give mobile phone / Gameboy to child two, who mimes talking / playing.)* He still needs looking after a bit by his mum and dad, but he's learning to cook and how to look after himself a bit more.

(Pointing to child three.) This is Lottie's mum, Sandra. She doesn't have a lot of time for toys or chatting on the phone, because she has to look after Lottie and Grant, and she also works in an office. *(Give clipboard to child three, who mimes writing on a clipboard.)* She also has to keep an eye on Grandpa, who lives on his own. Sandra is often tired because she has to work so hard. She needs a bit of peace and quiet now and then, after a hard day's work.

(Pointing to child four) And this is Lottie's Grandpa. He has quite a lot of peace and quiet because he doesn't work any more. He has a stick to help him walk because his legs are quite stiff. *(Give stick to child four, who mimes walking slowly with the aid of a stick.)* When he goes out shopping, he's sometimes a bit slow. He spends a lot of time sitting down, reading books and watching the television. He likes it when Sandra drops round with Lottie, because he finds his house a bit too quiet.

Have you noticed that all these people are different ages?

- Lottie is a baby.
- Grant is a teenager.
- Sandra is an adult.
- Grandpa is an old person.

Let's find out what makes them so different from each other.

INTERACTIVE FOLLOW UP ACTIVITIES

Questions

1) Who can spot some differences between these four people?
   (Open ended.)
2) Which one of them do you think does the most work?
   (Probably Sandra, because she has to look after Lottie and Grant, keep an eye on Grandpa and she has a job in an office.)
3) Who do you think sleeps the most?
   (Probably Lottie, because she still has a lot of growing to do and you need a lot of sleep to help you grow.)

Getting the message

Let's think about what we all need when we are at different ages.

1) What do you think baby Lottie's needs are?
   (She needs feeding, changing, dressing, playing with, talking to – so she can learn to talk herself – and keeping warm and safe.)
2) Does Grant need the same things as Lottie does?
   (No – he still needs food, but he can feed himself; he can also dress himself and get about on his own; he still needs people like his mum to look after him, but in a different way; he still needs somewhere warm and safe to live.)
3) Sandra needs different things too. Can you think of what she needs?
   (A job, so she can earn enough money to look after Lottie and Grant; she needs time to have a bit of a rest from all her hard work; she also needs a warm, safe place to live and food to eat.)
4) What about Grandpa?
   (He might need someone to help him with his cooking and cleaning, because he can't manage so well any more; he too still needs somewhere warm and safe to live; he also needs people to chat to, to stop him being lonely.)

Learning more

1) I'm going to tell you some things I think might be true. Give me a big thumbs-up, like this *(demonstrate)*, if you think I'm right. If you think I'm wrong, give me a big thumbs-down, like this *(demonstrate)*.

- We all change as we get older. *(T)*
- All old people walk with a stick. *(F)*
- Babies need a lot of looking after. *(T)*
- Only babies need clean clothes. *(F)*
- All old people do is watch the telly. *(F)*
- Adults who look after children have to work very hard. *(T)*

2) Can you think of anything that ALL of the people need, whether they are young or old, or in between? *(Food, shelter, company, etc.)*

NON-INTERACTIVE FOLLOW UP

Summary of the story

- Lottie is a baby.
- Grant is a teenager.
- Sandra is a working mum.
- Grandpa is an elderly person.
- Each of them has different needs.
- There are some things that all of them need, whether they are young or old.

Something to think about

1) Think about people who are older or younger than you. What sorts of things do they _all_ need, however old they are? What _different_ things do they need because of how old they are?
2) Do you need to treat people of different ages differently, or all the same?
3) You will change as you grow older. How will your life change as you grow up?

Reflection

Think carefully about how you treat people of different ages. People of all ages are important. Just because babies can't talk and old people aren't always very quick, doesn't mean that they are less important than older children or younger grown-ups.

Prayer

Lord God, thank you that we don't stay the same for all of our lives. Please help us to enjoy changing as we grow older. Also help us to get on with people of all ages. Amen.

3F USING HOUSEHOLD PRODUCTS SAFELY

Objective
To help children learn that household products, including medicines, can be harmful if not used properly.

PSHE/Citizenship links
3f (Household products)

Props
(Not essential): a bottle of bleach or another powerful cleaning substance. Alternatively you could bring in examples of as many of the products mentioned below as possible.

Introduction
It's amazing how many different things you can buy from a supermarket these days. There are hundreds and hundreds of different items: food, household products, toys, books, CDs and DVDs, electrical goods like microwaves, clothes – in fact, at a big supermarket you can buy almost anything. Household products are things we use around the home: you probably have cupboards in your house full of bottles and pots and jars and containers and boxes and aerosols and packets. But do you know that you need to be very careful with many of these things?

INFORMATION: TAKING CARE AT HOME

Let's start in the **kitchen**. In most kitchens there are quite a few things that need to be treated with real care. Sinks and cookers and floors all need cleaning and so you'll always find cleaning products in a kitchen. Some of these, like washing up liquid, are quite safe but there are other cleaning materials which can be harmful:

- Bleach is a very powerful cleaner which is only for grown-ups to use. Bleach comes in plastic bottles with a safety lid, which is very hard to open. It has this to stop children from opening the bottle.
- Dishwashers use strong chemicals for cleaning dirty plates and cups. Dishwasher cleaner can be a liquid in a bottle or a powder in a box or even in little square tablets. If you touch any of these you should wash your hands right away as they can make your skin red and itchy.
- Washing machines are just like dishwashers and use powder, liquid or tablet cleaners. Try not to touch these cleaners either.
- Some people keep boxes of matches in the kitchen. Never play with matches because they can burn you or start a fire. It's best to leave matches to adults.

Let's think about **bathrooms** next. There are things in most bathrooms that need to be treated with care too:

- All bathrooms need cleaning and so there are usually bottles and sprays in the room. Toilet cleaners use very strong chemicals to kill germs. These should only be used by grown ups, not children.

- Sometimes you will find sprays in bathrooms, like air fresheners. Try not to breathe in the spray from these, especially if you have asthma, as it isn't good for you.
- Some people keep medicines in a bathroom cupboard as well. There are all sorts of medicines: pills, tablets, liquids like Calpol, little plastic capsules, powders, creams, inhalers and sprays. Medicines can make you better but they can also harm you if you have the wrong ones or the wrong amount. Let a grown-up you know well give you the right medicines if you need them.

Some people keep medicines and other things which need careful handling in their **bedroom**:
- Nail varnish remover is a very strong chemical that you should not touch. It can even remove paint from doors, so it isn't good for your skin.
- Some hair products like dyes are made from dangerous chemicals, so it is best not to touch. There are always warnings on the label if they can be harmful.

Many products that need to be handled carefully are kept in **garages or sheds**. Some people keep them in utility rooms next to the kitchen too. So what might we find?
- Firelighters and barbecue lighters are used to start fires. These give off smelly fumes, which you can't see but which are not good for you to breathe in. Touching them is not good for your skin either.
- Fuels are chemicals which will catch fire. Petrol is very dangerous, and so are paraffin, white spirit and turpentine. All of these have a very strong smell, which usually means that you shouldn't go near them.
- Most garages have lots of other chemicals which you should leave to grown ups, like paint stripper, oil, wood stain, solvent glue, antifreeze and de-icer for the car.
- Some things are poisonous. Some people use poisons to get rid of mice or rats, or insects like ants and wasps. Weedkillers are very strong chemicals that you should not touch. All poisons have a large black X on the container.

So, there are many products in most people's houses, which have to be treated with a lot of care. But don't worry because they are all safe if you leave them to adults. You don't need to remember them all, either – if you're not sure if something is safe then you can do these three things:
1. Ask a grown up.
2. Look to see if there is a safety lid or a warning label on the container.
3. Leave it alone.

The message to remember is that all these things can be harmful, but only if they are not used properly.

INTERACTIVE FOLLOW UP ACTIVITIES

Questions
1) What are household products?
   (Things you buy for your home.)
2) Which kitchen products need to be handled carefully?
   (Kitchen cleaners, dishwasher and washing machine detergents, matches.)

3) Why do we need to be careful with medicines?

   (They can be harmful if they are not taken according to the instructions or if the wrong ones are taken.)

Getting the message

1) Why do some products have safety tops or warnings on the labels?

   (They can be harmful, e.g. if you get them on your skin or in your eyes or if you swallow them.)

2) Put your hand up if I mention a product which can be harmful:
   - Petrol ✓
   - Bleach ✓
   - Soap
   - Toilet cleaner ✓
   - Air freshener ✓
   - PVA Glue
   - Nail varnish remover ✓
   - Paraffin ✓
   - Olive oil

Learning more

1) How do people stop babies and toddlers getting hold of harmful household products?
2) Why are matches especially dangerous?

NON-INTERACTIVE FOLLOW UP

Summary of the assembly

- Household products are things that can be bought for the house.
- Some household products can be harmful if not used properly.
- In the kitchen, bleach, cleaners such as dishwasher tablets and matches can cause harm.
- In the bathroom, toilet cleaners, air fresheners and medicines must be handled carefully.
- Sheds and garages have fuels such as petrol, chemicals such as paint stripper and poisons such as weedkillers, which should not be touched by children at all.
- Dangerous substances have safety tops on the bottle or warning labels.

Something to think about

1) If a household product smells very strong, what does that usually mean?
2) Some glues give off dangerous fumes – are all glues like this?

Reflection

Be careful with household products around your home. Always ask before you use anything and watch out for safety tops and warning labels. Remember that even medicines can be harmful if not taken properly.

Prayer

Lord God, thank you that there are lots of useful household products that help us to clean our homes and do other jobs. Help us to be very careful with them and to use them properly. Please keep all of us safe. Amen.

3G RULES FOR KEEPING SAFE

Objective
To help children recognise rules for, and ways of, keeping safe and about people who can help them to stay safe.

PSHE/Citizenship links
3g (Rules)

Props
(Not essential): a dark coat, a light coat and a reflective armband

Introduction
Roads are very important to us all. We walk or drive along them every day: to the shops, to school, to our friends' houses and back home again. They are very useful, but they can also be really dangerous. It's up to us to learn how to use them safely. Listen carefully to this story about how two girls learnt a lot about road safety on their way home from school one dark afternoon in winter.

STORY: GOING HOME

It was nearly half past four and Gina and Helen had just been to recorder club after school. It was chilly and dark when they came out of the classroom. They put their coats on and skipped down the school path to where their mums were waiting at the gate.

The mums were having a very serious chat about something, and carried on talking as they all turned their backs on the school and started walking home. Gina and Helen ran on ahead. Helen's mum shouted, "Don't run too far ahead, girls, and be careful of the road!" and then went back to her conversation with Gina's mum.

The path that the girls were following had lots of cracks in the paving stones. They played the game where they pretended that bears would come out and eat them if they trod on any cracks. They kept giggling and laughing, because it was such good fun. "Aaagh!" shouted Helen. "The bears'll be coming to get us, 'cos you trod on a crack!"

"Quick!" laughed Gina. "We'll have to run, to escape!"

They grabbed each other's hands and both ran as fast as they could, away from the bears, laughing as they went. Suddenly all sorts of things happened very fast. They heard a scream from the mums behind them and a funny screeching sound in front of them; they saw a huge flash of lights right in front of them and heard a loud crunch, followed by the sound of a lot of glass breaking. For a minute everything went horribly quiet and then the girls heard their mums running towards them.

"What happened?" asked Gina, very frightened.

Helen began to cry, because the noise and the lights had scared her so much.

"Oh girls! Whatever were you thinking?" cried Gina's mum, hugging her very tight. "You just ran *straight* out into the road, without even looking! That car could have killed you!"

Now Gina began to cry, too.

"Oh my goodness," gasped Helen's mum, in a sort of scared voice, looking over to the car. "Is that driver OK, do you think?"

They all looked at the car that had just missed Gina and Helen. It had swerved off the road, gone straight through the low wall of someone's front garden and gone right into a greenhouse. The car was scratched and dented, and the greenhouse was just a heap of broken glass. The owner of the greenhouse came dashing out of her house to see what had happened. As she ran across the garden towards the car, the driver got out. He looked terrible: his face was as white as a sheet and his legs were all wobbly. He crunched his way across the broken glass to where the girls and their mums were standing. They were all crying and hugging each other.

"I'm so sorry..." began the driver. "I... I... just didn't see the children until it was too late. They just seemed to come out of nowhere, straight into the middle of the road. Are they alright?" His voice sounded just as wobbly as his legs looked – but he didn't sound one bit cross, just very scared and shocked.

After a minute or two, when everyone had calmed down a bit, they discovered that no one had actually been hurt. The garden wall had a huge hole in it, the car was a mess and the greenhouse was completely ruined, but all the grown-ups seemed to be worried about was whether everyone was OK or not. Even the lady whose greenhouse it was.

That night, Gina had a lovely deep, hot bath and her mum let her have some of her special, really expensive bubble bath that Dad had bought her for her birthday. She stayed with Gina the whole time and Gina was sure that she saw her wipe a tear out of her eyes a couple of times. She had extra cuddles from her mum and her dad at bedtime, and went to bed with a special hot water bottle and had an extra long story read to her. As Mum kissed her goodnight, she said, "Have a good night's sleep, Gina, and tomorrow I think that we need to have a big talk, don't you? Goodnight, sweetheart."

Gina felt all cosy and warm and safe as she drifted off to sleep, and she knew exactly what mum wanted to talk about in the morning.

INTERACTIVE FOLLOW UP ACTIVITIES

Questions
1) Why were Gina and Helen coming out of school so late that day?
   (They'd been to recorder club.)
2) What was it like when they came out of the school?
   (Cold and dark.)
3) Were they walking home on their own?
   (No; their mums were there to walk them home, but they were having a chat so they didn't pay too much attention to the girls.)

Getting the message
1) What do you think that Gina's mum wanted to talk to her about in the morning?
   (Road safety.)
2) Did the girls' mums tell them to be careful while they were walking home?
   (Yes, they said, "Don't run too far ahead, girls, and be careful of the road!")
3) Why do you think the girls didn't do what they were told? Put your hand up when you hear the right reason:
   - They were very bad girls, who decided to be naughty and didn't want to do what they were told. *(F)*

71

- They wanted to get home as fast as they could. *(F)*
- They just forgot, because they were having fun playing a game. *(T)*

Learning more

1) What mistakes did the girls make on their way home?
   (Running along, not looking where they were going. Not stopping at the side of the road and waiting for their mums to help them cross the road.)

2) Here is a coat like the one that both of the girls wore that night *(hold up a dark coat)*. What can you tell me about it? *(It's dark.)* Why does the dark colour make it dangerous to walk home in, on a dark night?
   (Drivers and other road users can't see you when you're wearing dark clothes.)

3) What could you do, so that drivers can see you better? Give me a thumbs-up or a thumbs-down for these ideas:
   - Wear a light coloured coat. ✓
   - Scream loudly at cars as they come near you.
   - If you already have a dark coat, wear reflective armbands *(hold up example & explain how they work)*. ✓
   - Carry a torch if you're walking in the dark. ✓
   - Wear a light coloured hat, gloves and scarf. ✓
   - Just run home REALLY fast.

4) Hands up who can think of people who can help us stay safe on the roads?
   (Police officers, lollipop ladies, parents, teachers, etc.)

NON-INTERACTIVE FOLLOW UP

Summary of the story
- Gina and Helen were going home one cold, dark afternoon.
- Their mums told them to mind the road.
- The girls played a game and forgot to be careful.
- A car nearly hit them, because they ran into the middle of the road without looking.
- No one was hurt, but there was a lot of damage and everyone was very frightened.

Something to think about
1) What sort of road safety rules can you think of?
2) Is it safe to cross a road on your own?
3) Make sure that you wear clothes that people can see in the dark.

Reflection
Make sure that you are always very careful when you are near roads. Cars can travel very fast and find it difficult to stop in a hurry. Never mess around or play games near roads and always cross roads with a grown up.

Prayer
Lord God, thank you for roads and cars, and how useful they are to us. Please help us to stay safe on the roads. Help us not to mess about when we are near cars and help us to think carefully about crossing roads safely. Amen.

4A How Our Behaviour Affects Others

Objective
To help children to recognise how their behaviour affects other people.

PSHE/Citizenship links
4a (How behaviour affects people)

Props
(Not essential): a large teddy bear

Introduction
None of us can be happy and cheerful all the time, but next time you're feeling very cross or grumpy, have a think how your bad mood can make other people feel. Listen carefully to this story by an author called John Richardson and see if you can spot the ways that this teddy bear's mood spoilt the day for everyone he met.

Story: Bad Mood Bear

"Good night," said Mum.

"Good night," said Dad.

But Bear didn't go to sleep. First he played with his soldiers, then he read his picture book and then he tiptoed out onto the landing to listen to the noise of the television. Soon he began to feel thirsty. He went downstairs to ask for a glass of water.

"You'll be tired tomorrow," warned Dad.

At breakfast next morning, Bear threw his porridge on the floor.

"Goodness me!" said Grandma Bear.

"Good heavens!" said Mum and Dad together.

But Bear just growled. "I'm in a bad mood," he said. Mum gathered Bad Mood Bear up in her arms and took him out into the garden. She put him on the swing to cheer him up. But Bear had a tantrum. He fell over backwards and bumped his head.

"Stupid swing," said Bear, bursting into tears.

"Let me rub your bump better," said Mum.

"Leave me alone, you!" screamed Bear.

So Mum did.

As soon as Mum was gone, he picked up a big stick and hit the swing as hard as he could. What a bad mood bear!

Bear could see Grandma and Grandad watching him from the window. He poked his tongue out at them. "That bear needs a good smack," said Grandad. Grandma agreed.

"Hello, Bear," said the pigs from next door. "This is our new friend, Goat."

"So what!" snarled Bear.

"We're going down to the river to play, are you coming?"

"No, you don't play properly," replied Bear rudely.

Goat said the Bear wasn't very nice and they were better off without him.

"He's not our friend any more," said Pig.

Bear mooched around, kicking stones and growling. A fly buzzed around his nose. "Buzz off!" screamed Bear, flapping his arms around in a temper.

Grandad was gardening in the vegetable patch and laughed to see Bear jumping around in such a rage. "Bad Mood Bear, calm down and stop making such a fuss!" he called out. And do you know what Bear did? That bad mood bear ran over and kicked Grandad's leg!

"Ouch!" shouted Grandad as he fell over.

Dad rushed out angrily. He grabbed Bear by the ear, took him up to his bedroom and smacked his bottom. "We've had enough of your bad mood," he said. "Behave yourself!"

Bad Mood Bear screamed and screamed. He screamed so hard that his throat hurt and his eyes ran. Then he pulled a few rude faces, but it wasn't much fun when there was no one there to see them.

Later on, Mum brought Bad Mood Bear a glass of milk and a biscuit. Outside a bee was humming in a sleepy sort of way. Bad Mood Bear yawned; very soon he began to feel tired. Mum closed the curtains. Within seconds Bad Mood Bear was asleep.

Bear slept for a long, long time. When he woke up he smiled his first smile of the day.

At lunchtime when Mum gave Bear his fish fingers he said, "Thank you," very politely, and ate them all up. After he had licked the bowl clean he thought about all the naughty things he had done that morning. "I'm sorry I was a bad mood bear," he said.

Later on Bear joined his friends at the river. "Can I play too?" he asked.

"Only if you promise not to be in a bad mood," said Pig.

"I promise," said Bear.

And he was a good mood bear all afternoon.

[BAD MOON BEAR by John Richardson, published by Hutchinson. Used by permission of the Random House Group Limited.]

INTERACTIVE FOLLOW UP ACTIVITIES

Questions

1) What did Bear do instead of going to sleep when he should have done, at the beginning of the story?
   (He played with his soldiers, read his picture book and went onto the landing to listen to the noise of the television.)

2) Can you remember the very first naughty thing Bear did when he got up the next morning?
   (He threw his porridge onto the floor.)

3) Who was Bear rude to during his Bad Mood Day?
   (Mum: shouted at her, Grandma & Grandad: stuck his tongue out at them, the pigs and Goat: told them they didn't play properly.)

4) Bear was in such a bad mood, he even hurt someone. Can you remember who that was?
   (Grandad: he kicked him and Grandad fell over.)

Getting the message

1) Why was Bear in such a bad mood that morning?
   (He was too tired.)

2) Imagine you are the other people in the story. How do you think they all felt about what Bear was doing? Ask for volunteers to come and explain how they would feel.
   - Mum: (*sad because she tried to cheer bear up even though he was being horrid*).
   - Dad: (*very angry, especially after Bear kicked Grandad*).
   - Grandma and Granddad: (*very shocked, especially when he poked his tongue out at them and kicked Grandad*).
   - Pigs: (*very surprised and hurt that he said that they didn't play properly*).
   - Goat: (*wouldn't want to make friends with such a grumpy bear*).

Learning more

1) When Bear woke up he felt much better. What good things did he do when he got up from his sleep?
   (*Ate his meal nicely, instead of throwing it on the floor; **said he was sorry**; was nice to his friends.*)
2) How did the other people in the story help Bear?
   (*Dad put a stop to him behaving so badly; Mum helped him to calm down and helped him get to sleep; his friends were kind to him and let him play with them, even though he'd been so rude to them.*)

NON-INTERACTIVE FOLLOW UP

Summary of the story
- Bear doesn't go to sleep when he should, so he's very tired the next day.
- He's in a bad mood all morning and does some very naughty things.
- He throws his breakfast on the floor, has a tantrum, hits the swing, shouts at his mum, pokes his tongue out at his grandparents, kicks Grandad, screams a lot and is rude to his friends.
- When he calms down, he goes to sleep and feels much better.
- He's in a good mood for the rest of the day and says that he's sorry.

Something to think about
1) Do you ever get into a bad mood?
2) What could you do, if you're in a bad mood, to stop yourself being horrid to those around you?
3) If you slip up and behave badly after all, what can you do afterwards to try and make things right again?

Reflection
We all get grumpy now and again, but we must all try to make sure that we don't upset other people by our bad behaviour. (That goes for grown-ups as well as children!)

Prayer
Lord God, thank you for friends and families. Help us to be nice and kind to those around us, however we feel inside. If we make a mistake and get into a bad mood with people, please forgive us, and help us to go and say sorry to those people we have upset or hurt. Amen.

4B LISTENING TO OTHERS

Objective
To help children appreciate the value of listening to others and co-operating.

PSHE/Citizenship links
4b (Listening to others)

Props
(Not essential): a teddy bear

Introduction
Everyone knows what a teddy is, but how many people know how teddy bears got their name? It's a very interesting story – a story we can all learn from.

TRUE STORY: THE FIRST TEDDY

Margarete Steiff had been very poorly when she was a young girl growing up in Germany. Now that she was grown up, Margarete needed a wheelchair to move around but she was a bright talented person who wanted to make the most of her life.

Margarete was very good at sewing and she decided to become a dressmaker. She made clothes for people in her town and made them very well. But sometimes, there were quiet days when no one wanted any clothes made or mended. It was on one of these quiet days that Margarete had an idea. She was wondering if she could make anything from the leftover scraps of material in her workroom.

Margarete thought a soft animal would be a good thing to make so she cut out the shape of an elephant in two pieces and stuffed it with padding. She sewed the two parts together and added eyes and ears. It looked really good.

Margarete made some more soft animals and showed them to a little girl who was visiting her.

"Oh they're lovely – can I have one?" asked the girl.

"Of course," said Margarete. This gave her an idea. She started sewing all sorts of zoo animals like lions and giraffes, as well as pets like cats and dogs. Margarete gave these away as presents and they were very popular.

All of Margarete's soft toys were beautifully made and often people who saw them went to ask Margarete if they could buy one from her. Margarete decided to start making the toys to sell: she opened a small factory and found some other people who could help her with the sewing. Soon things were going very well – word got about that Margarete Steiff made wonderful toy animals and people travelled from all over Europe to buy them.

One day, Margarete's nephew brought her a drawing of a bear he had done at the zoo. Margarete had never made a bear before but she set to work. But people didn't like the bear and no one bought it so Margarete changed the bear's shape to make it more cuddly. It worked – soon people were buying bears along with the other animals and Margarete had to move into a bigger factory to make more toys.

People were now coming to buy Margarete's animals from all over the world and one particular toy buyer from America adored the little cuddly bear.

"I'd like to buy some bears from you," he said.

"Of course," replied Margarete. "How many?"

"Three thousand."

It was by far the biggest order Margarete had ever had. Everyone at the factory worked long and hard to make the 3000 bears to go to the USA.

Just at this time in America, the United States' President heard some good news. His daughter was getting married. The president decided to have a big meal to celebrate, with over a hundred people invited. The president's name was Theodore Roosevelt but everyone called him Teddy for short.

The man who was organising the special celebration meal for the President's daughter was very busy. He needed to get everything ready: food, plates, waiters and waitresses, knives and forks, and something special to decorate the tables – something really unusual and fun for this happy occasion. He was passing a toyshop window when he saw a little toy bear - it was one of Margarete's 3000 bears, which had gone to be sold in America. The man thought the bear would make a great table decoration so he went into the shop and bought several.

When the day of the celebration meal arrived, the long tables looked wonderful. On each one were several bears, dressed up in costumes – sailor bears, soldier bears, camping bears, fishing bears – all sorts. The meal was a great success and so were the bears.

"What do you call these bears?" someone asked President Teddy Roosevelt.

"I don't know – they're new to me!" he replied.

Then a guest said, "They must be 'Teddy Bears'!"

Soon, everyone was talking about Teddy Bears, including the newspapers who were reporting on the special meal. Before long, everyone wanted one of these cuddly bears and toy makers all over the world began to make them.

Just think about it: there might not ever have been any teddies at all, if Margarete hadn't listened to the people who liked her zoo animals. Or if she hadn't listened to her nephew, or to the people who wanted her to make bears. And what if the President hadn't listened to the man who wanted to put bears on the tables at his dinner, or if no one had listened to the guest who first called them Teddy Bears? It's a good job they did listen, isn't it?!

INTERACTIVE FOLLOW UP ACTIVITIES

Questions

1) What was Margarete Steiff good at?

   (Sewing and listening to people!)

2) Where did she get the idea for making a bear?

   (From her nephew.)

3) Where did the name Teddy come from?

   (It was the name everyone called the US President, Theodore Roosevelt.)

Put your thumb up if I say something true about this story:

- Margarete was from Germany. ✓
- Margarete thought of the name teddy bears.
- Margarete was disabled. ✓
- Margarete listened to other people and this helped her. ✓
- The President of America didn't like the bears.

What can we learn from this story?

We can learn that listening to others can help you to do things really well.

NON-INTERACTIVE FOLLOW UP

Summary of the story

- Margarete Steiff grew up in Germany.
- Margarete was disabled but she was clever and very good at sewing.
- Margarete made soft toy zoo animals to give away as presents.
- Margarete's nephew gave her the idea for making a bear.
- Lots of people bought her toys.
- A man bought 3000 bears and took them to America.
- The bears were given the name 'Teddy Bears' after the US President, Teddy Roosevelt.

Something to think about

1) Try hard to listen to other people.
2) Listening to others can give you all sorts of good ideas.
3) If you want people to listen to you, you need to listen to other people.

Reflection

Learn from the story of Margarete Steiff, who listened to others, worked hard and made something that everyone loves.

Prayer

Lord God, help me to be a good listener, like Margarete Steiff in Germany. Help me to encourage others, like people encouraged her – and thank you for teddy bears too! Amen.

4c Respecting Differences

Objective
To help children respect the differences between people.

PSHE/Citizenship links
4c (Differences between people)

Props
(Not essential): a soft toy and a picture book of *Ruby* by Maggie Glen

Introduction
All of us are different. We have different coloured eyes, skin and hair; some of us are tall, some of us are short; some of us wear glasses, some of us don't; some of us find school work easy, some of us don't; some of us can run fast, some of us can't run at all. But ALL of us are special in some way. Listen to this story about a VERY special bear called Ruby.

Story: Ruby

Ruby felt different from other bears – sort of special. Mrs Harris had been day-dreaming when she made Ruby. She didn't notice that she'd used the spotted material that was meant for the toy leopards. She didn't watch carefully when she sewed on the nose.

Ruby wasn't surprised when she was chosen from the other bears, but she didn't like being picked up by her ear.

"OUCH, GET OFF!" she growled. Ruby's paw was stamped with an 'S' and she was thrown into the air. "YIPEE-E-E-E! 'S' IS FOR 'SPECIAL'," yelled Ruby.

Ruby flew across the factory and landed in a box full of bears.

"Hello," she said. "My name's Ruby and I'm special – see." She held up her paw.

"No, silly," laughed a big bear. 'S' is for 'second' – second best."

"We're mistakes," said the bear with rabbit ears. "When the box is full, we'll all be thrown out."

Ruby's fur stood on end; she was horrified.

Ruby decided to help all of the toys with 'S' printed on their paws to escape and she ended up in the window of the very best toy shop in town.

The other toys stared at Ruby.

"What's the 'S' for?" squealed the pigs.

"Special," said Ruby proudly.

All the toys shrieked with laughter.

"Scruffy," said the smart-looking penguin.

"Soppy," said the chimpanzee.

"Stupid," giggled the mice.

"Very strange for a bear," they all agreed.

"Don't come next to me," said a prim doll.

"Wouldn't want to," said Ruby.

"Stand at the back," shouted the other toys.

They poked, they pulled, they prodded and they pinched. Ruby pushed back as hard as she could, but there were too many of them. So Ruby spent all day at the back of the shelf.

Then, just before closing time, a small girl came into the shop with her grandfather.

They searched and searched for something – something different, something special.

"That's the one," said the little girl.

"Yes, Susie," said Grandfather, "that one looks very special."

Ruby looked around her. "Can they see me? IT'S ME! They're pointing at me. WHOOPEE-E-E-E!"

"We'll have that one, please," said Grandfather.

The shopkeeper put Ruby on the counter.

She looked at the 'S' on Ruby's paw.

"I'm sorry, sir," she said. "This one is a second. I'll fetch another."

"No thank you, that one is just perfect," said Grandfather. "It has character."

Character, thought Ruby, that sounds good.

"Shall I wrap it for you?" the shopkeeper asked.

"Not likely," growled Ruby. "Who wants to be shoved in a paper bag?"

"No thank you," said Susie. "I'll have her just as she is."

They all went out of the shop and down the street.

When they came to a yellow door they stopped.

"We're home, Spotty," said Susie.

"SPOTTY, WHAT A CHEEK!" muttered Ruby.

"It's got a growl," said Susie, and she and her grandfather laughed.

Susie took off her coat and scarf and sat Ruby on her lap.

Susie stared at Ruby and Ruby stared back.

Suddenly Ruby saw a little silver 'S' hanging on a chain round Susie's neck.

"Hooray!" thought Ruby. "One of us – a special."

[Extract from RUBY by Maggie Glen, published by Hutchinson. Used by permission of the Random House Group Limited.]

INTERACTIVE FOLLOW UP ACTIVITIES

Questions

1) How was Ruby different from all of the other bears in the factory?
   (She was made with spotty fabric that should have been used to make a leopard and the person sewing on her nose hadn't been watching carefully, so it was wonky.)

2) What did the people at the factory put onto Ruby's paw?
   (They printed an 'S' on it.)

3) What did the 'S' stand for?
   (Second, or second best.)

4) What did Ruby think the 'S' stood for?
   (She thought it meant 'special'.)

Getting the message

1) Put your hand up if you think that the other toys in the toy shop window were kind to Ruby.

2) Put your hand up if you thought they were mean.

   (Yes – they called her names and made her stand at the very back of the window.)

3) Can you remember some of the things they said Ruby's 'S' on her paw stood for?

   (Scruffy, Soppy, Stupid, Strange.)

4) When Grandfather and Susie saw her, what did they think of Ruby?

   (They thought she was special; they wanted something a bit different.)

Learning more

1) Imagine that someone a bit different comes into your classroom. What would be the right thing to do? Put your thumbs up if you think each one of these is a good idea and your thumbs down if you think it's a bad idea:

   • Gang up with your friends and laugh at them.

   • Be friendly to them and help them to feel at home.

   • Call them names.

   • Ask them to join in your games and help them if they don't know what to do.

NON-INTERACTIVE FOLLOW UP

Summary of the story

• Ruby isn't made just like all the other bears and she is labelled as 'second best'.

• She thinks she's 'special'.

• Ruby goes to a toy shop and all the other toys are mean to her because she looks different.

• Susie and her grandfather love the way that Ruby is different from all the other toys.

• They choose her because they think she's very special.

Something to think about

1) How do you treat people who are a bit different?

2) Is it kind to call people names because they are different?

3) Remember that ALL of us are different and special in some way or another.

Reflection

If you feel different from other people in some way, don't worry. Remember how different Ruby was. She knew that she was special and she found a friend who liked her because she was a bit different.

Prayer

Lord God, thank you that you made us all different from each other and that you made us all special. Help me to understand that people who are different from me aren't worse than me, or better – just different. Help us all to get along and be kind to one another. Amen.

4D CARING FOR EACH OTHER

Objective
To help children learn that family and friends should care for each other.

PSHE/Citizenship links
4d (Caring for each other)

Props
(Not essential): a torch

Introduction
Most of the time we can look after ourselves, but there are times when we can't. Sometimes we need someone else to look after us and to take care of us. When we're poorly, or if we've had an accident, we may need lots of care. Today's assembly features part of a story about a boy called Danny who lives with his father. Danny's father has had a rather nasty accident when he was out in the woods at night and Danny has gone to look for him.

STORY EXTRACT: DANNY FINDS HIS FATHER

I kept the torch on and went deeper into the wood.

"Dad!" I shouted. "Dad! It's Danny! Are you there?"

I didn't know which direction I was going in. I just went on walking and calling out, walking and calling; and each time I called I would stop and listen. But no answer came.

After a time, my voice began to go all trembly. I started to say silly things like, "Oh Dad, please tell me where you are! Please answer me! Please, oh please..." And then I knew that if I wasn't careful, the sheer hopelessness of it all would get the better of me and I would simply give up and lie down under the trees.

"Are you there, Dad? Are you there?" I shouted. "It's Danny!"

I stood still, listening, listening, listening, and in the silence that followed, I heard or thought I heard the faint, but oh so faint, sound of a human voice.

I froze and kept listening.

Yes, there it was again.

I ran towards the sound. "Dad!" I shouted. "It's Danny! Where are you?"

I stopped again and listened.

This time the answer came just loud enough for me to hear the words. "I'm here!" the voice called out. "Over here!"

It was him!

I was so excited my legs began to get all shaky.

"Where are you, Danny?" my father called out.

"I'm here, Dad! I'm coming."

With the beam of the torch shining ahead of me, I ran towards the voice. The trees were bigger here and spaced farther apart. The ground was a carpet of brown leaves from last year and it was good to run on. I didn't call out any more after that. I simply dashed ahead.

And all at once, his voice was right in front of me. "Stop, Danny, stop!" he shouted.

82

I stopped dead. I shone the torch over the ground. I couldn't see him.

"Where are you, Dad?"

"I'm down here. Come forward slowly. But be careful. Don't fall in."

I crept forward. Then I saw the pit. I went to the edge of it and shone the light downward and there was my father. He was sitting on the floor of the pit and looked up into the light and said, "Hello, my marvellous darling. Thank you for coming."

"Are you all right, Dad?"

"My ankle seems to be broken," he said. "It happened when I fell in."

The pit had been dug in the shape of a square with each side about six feet long. But it was the depth of it that was so awful. It was at least twelve feet deep. The sides had been cut straight down into the earth, presumably with a mechanical shovel, and no man could have climbed out of it without help.

"Does it hurt?" I asked.

"Yes," he said. "It hurts a lot. But don't worry about that. The point is, I've got to get out of here before morning. The keepers know I'm here and they're coming back for me as soon as it gets light."

"Did they dig the hole to catch people?" I asked.

"Yes," he said.

I shone my light around the top of the pit and saw how the keeper had covered it over with sticks and leaves and how the thing had collapsed when my father had stepped on it. It was the kind of trap hunters in Africa dig to catch wild animals.

"Do the keepers know who you are?" I asked.

"No," he said. "Two of them came and shone a light down on me but I covered my face with my arms and they couldn't recognize me. I heard them trying to guess. They were guessing all sorts of names but they didn't mention mine. Then one of them shouted, "We'll find out who you are all right in the morning, my lad."

Danny manages to get his father out of the pit using a rope and they return home to safety before morning.

[Extract from *Danny The Champion of the World* by Roald Dahl, Jonathan Cape Ltd & Penguin Books Ltd. Reproduced by permission of David Higham Associates.]

INTERACTIVE FOLLOW UP ACTIVITIES

Questions

1) Why did Danny go into the woods at night?

   (To find his father.)

2) What had happened to Danny's father?

   (He had fallen down a pit and broken his ankle.)

3) How can we tell that Danny really cares about his father?

   (He is worried about him; he goes out at night in a dark, dangerous place; he is very relieved to find him.)

Getting the message

1) Danny's father was really stuck in the pit and he needed help to get out. Sometimes we get stuck with things and we need help. We sometimes get stuck with our work at school and get help from the teacher. Or at home we might be feeling poorly, or upset about one of our friends.

Sometimes we need to help other people in our families when they are stuck too. Put your hand up if you have helped someone in your family who was stuck with something. *(Ask a few children to share their experiences.)*

2) We will probably never need to pull our parents out of a deep hole in the ground, but there are lots of other ways we can help them. I'm going to say some things you can do at home and you can give them a thumbs-up if they are helpful and thumbs-down if they are not helpful:

- Tidying your bedroom – is that helpful?
- Saying please and thank you.
- Leaving your clothes in a pile on the floor.
- Talking about what you've done at school.
- Saying sorry if you've been naughty.
- Arguing with your parents.

Learning more

1) What other helpful things can we do at home to show that we care for our parents?
2) Do you agree with these? *Ask for 3 volunteers – good readers – to read out these statements:*

- If you want people to care for you, you need to care for other people.
- You can show that you care by helping someone.
- A person who cares is careful about what they say.

NON-INTERACTIVE FOLLOW UP

Summary of the sory

- Danny's father went to the woods at night but didn't come back.
- Danny went out into the dark woods to look for him, using a torch.
- Danny spent a long time searching and calling – he was very scared and worried.
- Danny eventually heard his father's voice and found out he had fallen into a deep pit.
- The pit had been dug by keepers to trap people.
- Danny's father had broken his ankle and was in a lot of pain, but he knew that Danny could help him now that he'd found him.

Something to think about

1) Danny showed he really cared about his father by going to look for him in a dark, scary wood. There are lots of little, far easier ways that we can show we care for people too.
2) Are you helpful at home? That shows that you care.
3) Being polite, listening and saying please and thank you also shows that you care.

Reflection

Care for the people who care for you. Be helpful and kind; think about how you can do something to cheer someone up each day, especially your parents when they are tired.

Prayer

Lord God, thank you that there are lots of people who take care of me. Please help me to be a caring person who thinks about others. Please help me to care for the people in my family by being kind and helpful. Help me to remember to say thank you for all the care I get. Amen.

4E BULLYING

Objective
To help children understand what bullying is and how to respond to it.

PSHE/Citizenship links
4e (Teasing and bullying)

Props
None

Introduction
Today's assembly is all about bullying. Bullying is a very serious thing, but it's important that we all understand exactly what it is. We also need to know what to do about it. Today's story will help...

STORY: MUM'S BULLY

"Mum," said Carl. "I'm being bullied at school. Our teacher said that we should tell someone if we're being bullied."

Carl, who was seven years old, was sitting eating his breakfast. His mum put down the letter she was reading and looked at him.

"Well you'd better tell me about it then – what happened?"

"It was last week. There's this new girl in our class and she's really mean to everyone. She's bigger than me too and she pushed me at playtime when we were lining up to go inside."

"Oh, I see. Were you hurt?" said Mum.

"Well she pushed me quite hard but I didn't fall over."

"Right; and has she pushed you again or done anything else to you?"

"Err no, not to me, but I saw her calling Maggie Grainger names and she pushed Alex once too, when we were playing football."

"Well Carl, it doesn't sound like you've been bullied to me," said Mum, smiling gently.

"But Mum, you haven't seen this girl, she's horrid!"

"What's this horrid girl's name then?"

"She's called Regan."

"That's an unusual name," said Mum. "But anyway Carl, I need to explain to you why you can't really call this bullying. You see, a bully does something to a person more than once. If Regan had been pushing you lots and lots or if she'd been picking on you for over a week or two, say, then that would be different."

"But she did push me hard Mum."

"It's OK Carl, I believe you, but I bet you've pushed people at school sometimes, haven't you?"

"Well, only once or twice if they've been really annoying me."

"I see – so does that mean you're a bully?"

"No, course not Mum!"

"Right, that wasn't bullying; bullying is when someone hurts or upsets another person several times over a period of days or weeks."

"You mean when a kid picks on another kid a lot."

"That's right. You can't call every push or shove or even a fight bullying unless it keeps happening to the same person. Pushing and shoving is still wrong, and a very bad thing to do – it's just not always the same as bullying."

"How come you know so much about bullying then Mum?"

"I'll tell you when you come home from school Carl – it's already half eight, so we'd better get going."

At first playtime that day, Carl kept a special eye out for Regan to see what she was up to. Regan was standing on her own when Carl saw her, leaning against a netball post. She looked a bit miserable and Carl wondered if she was lonely. "Perhaps no one's been playing with her," thought Carl. Then two other girls from Carl's class went running past Regan and said something to her. He couldn't hear the words but it looked like they were making fun of her. It was probably because she was so tall.

Carl forgot about Regan for the rest of the day, but when he got home he told his mum about what he'd seen in the playground.

"Maybe those girls were bullying Regan," she said.

"But Mum, they didn't touch her, they just said something to her."

"Well, that can be a type of bullying too you know Carl – but only if someone keeps on doing it, remember."

"What, you mean calling people names can be bullying?"

"Yes – it happened to me when I was about your age."

"What happened?"

"Well, there was this boy who kept picking on me for some reason – I think it was because in those days I had lots of freckles and bright ginger hair. He called me rude names and made fun of me in front of his friends."

"What did you do?"

"Well, at first I didn't do anything – everyone gets called names at school I thought, so I tried to ignore him."

"Did he stop then?"

"No, he didn't. Things became worse. He used swear words and teased me on the way to school and got all his friends to call me nasty names too. It really upset me – he did it for months and months."

"Didn't you tell anyone?"

"At first I didn't – children in those days said you were soft if you told a teacher about something like that. But it got so bad that I didn't want to go to school. My father noticed that I wasn't eating properly as well and he started asking me about it. At first I said there was nothing wrong, but after a while I told him all about the boy."

"What did he do, Mum?"

"He went to see my teacher and the whole thing was sorted out. My teacher was really helpful and the boy was sent to the headmaster of the school. I don't know what the headmaster said to him but he stopped calling me names."

"That's good – were you ever bullied again?"

"No, but I helped some of my friends who were bullied. You see, I really should have told someone much earlier about what happened to me – it would have saved me months of misery. So I helped other children who were being bullied after that."

"How did you help them?"

"I just explained what had happened to me and said that they needed to tell a teacher and their parents. Sometimes I told the teacher if they were scared to."

"So what kind of bullying was going on?"

"Well, there are all kinds of bullying: there's the physical kind like hitting and kicking and pushing and fighting and pinching or tripping and that kind of thing. Then there's bullying using words, which is what happened to me: name calling, teasing, laughing at other children a lot, being rude or swearing. But there are also other kinds of bullying, which can hurt people just as much."

"What's that Mum?"

"Well, things like spreading lies and rumours; or leaving people out of things and ignoring them on purpose, or turning people's friends away from them."

"Hey – I think that's what was happening to Regan a bit. She was getting called names, but the other girls were leaving her out too."

"Maybe you're right Carl. Perhaps that's why she was pushing other people sometimes – she's probably lonely and fed up with being left out. Why don't you talk to her and make friends?"

"But Mum, she's a girl!"

"Oh Carl..."

INTERACTIVE FOLLOW UP ACTIVITIES

Questions

1) Was Carl being bullied by Regan?

   (No because she only pushed him once.)

2) What sort of things did Carl's mum say could be counted as bullying?

   (Physical things such as kicking etc, using words e.g. name-calling and indirect things such as spreading lies and leaving people out.)

3) Why did Mum think that Regan was pushing people?

   (Because she was being treated badly herself and left out by the other girls.)

Show of hands

- Who thinks bullying is wrong?
- Who will tell a teacher or a parent or a friend if they are being bullied?

Types of bullying

Some things are bullying and some are not. Call out yes or no to these questions (no shouting, though!):

- If a person calls you a name just once, is that bullying? *(No)*
- If someone keeps upsetting someone else, is that bullying? *(Yes)*
- Do bullies always hit or kick or push people? *(No)*
- Do bullies sometimes use words and names to hurt people? *(Yes)*
- Is a bully a person who picks on another person lots of times? *(Yes)*
- Is it best to tell someone if you think you are being bullied? *(Yes)*
- Should you tell your teacher every time you get just a tiny bit upset about something? *(No)*

NON-INTERACTIVE FOLLOW UP

Summary of the story

- Carl told his mum he had been bullied.
- He said that a new girl had pushed him once.
- Carl's mum explained that this wasn't bullying because bullying was when the same person hurt or upset you lots of times.
- Mum explained how she'd been bullied at school.
- Mum's bullying stopped when she told her dad, who told her teacher.
- Mum explained that there are lots of different types of bullying, including physical bullying, using words and leaving people out, or talking about people in nasty ways.

Something to think about

1) Do you ever pick on people?
2) Who should you tell if you think you are being bullied?

Reflection

Sometimes, if you are being bullied, you might be frightened to tell someone, but it's very important that you do, so that the bullying can be stopped. So be brave. Also watch out for other people being bullied and make sure that you don't pick on people yourself.

Prayer

Lord God, thank you that there are people we can turn to for help if we are being bullied. Please help bullies to stop what they are doing and treat people kindly. Help us not to use bad names or to tease and upset other people. Help us to be brave, to tell a grown-up if we are being bullied, or if we see someone else being bullied. Amen.

Badger Publishing Limited
26 Wedgwood Way, Pin Green Industrial Estate,
Stevenage, Hertfordshire SG1 4QF
Telephone: 01438 356907
Fax: 01438 747015
www.badger-publishing.co.uk
enquiries@badger-publishing.co.uk

Badger Assembly Stories with Citizenship and PSHE themes
Ages 5-7
ISBN 1 84424 229 3

Publisher: David Jamieson
Editor: Paul Martin
Designer: Adam Wilmott

Printed in the UK.